I0169478

The Totally Unauthorized OBAMACARE Joke Book

Created, Collected and Edited

by

Tim Barry

The Totally Unauthorized Obamacare Joke Book™
Copyright © 2013 by Timothy Barry. All rights reserved.

Printed in the United States of America.

No part of this book may be used or reproduced in whole or part without written permission except in the case of reprints in the context of reviews. For information contact IT Press, P.O. Box 871016, Vancouver, WA 98687.

website: www.obamacarejokebook.com

10 9 8 7 6 5 4 3 2

ISBN: 978-0-9667417-3-5 (Paperback Edition)

ISBN: 978-0-9667417-4-2 (Amazon Kindle Edition)

ISBN: 978-0-9667417-5-9 (ePub Edition)

ISBN: 978-0-9667417-6-6 (PDF Edition)

This book is not authorized by or associated in any way with the Republican Party, the Democratic party, any other political party, The Patient Protection and Affordable Care Act, any products or any of the other companies, products or individuals mentioned herein. Any factual items are specifically identified. Other than items specifically identified as factual ,all quotes, anecdotes, scenarios and other items are works of fiction, satire and parody and none of these fictional items should be assumed to be in any way true or accurate and any resemblance between these fictional items and any true or actual events is unintentional and purely co-incidental.

The Totally Unauthorized Obamacare Joke Book™ and The Totally Unauthorized Joke Book™ series are trademarks of IT-Press

Any and all other trademarks or quotes used herein are hereby acknowledged as the property of their respective owners.

Cover design by George Foster
Copy editing by Lilja Toban-Finzel and Janet A. Fallon

Table of Contents

The Totally Unauthorized Obamacare Joke Book

"Laughter and tears are both responses to frustration and exhaustion... I myself prefer to laugh, since there is less cleaning up to do afterward." - Kurt Vonnegut, Jr.

1.0   Introduction

The Patient Protection and Affordable Care Act, aka "Obamacare", has been controversial from the start. Following heated debate and razor thin votes in both the U.S. House of Representatives and Senate it was finally signed into law by President Obama on March 23, 2010.

Bringing major changes to the healthcare of millions of Americans is a massive undertaking and the debate surrounding Obamacare has continued unabated fueled by the less than stellar launch of the Healthcare.gov website. Obamacare is just plain too big, too expensive and, well, too visible to not make a really great target for all kinds of jokes.

This is a collection of humor about Obamacare. The law. The website. President Obama and his administration. Republicans and Democrats. Senators and Representatives. Insurance companies. Consultants. Nobody gets a pass. Jokes, mock news stories, top ten lists, poems, groaners, songs and more. Some jokes are timely adaptations of old classic jokes but many are original and have never been published before; some of the items are actually true! Many items are laced with appearances by famous people and jokes about other current events further liven up the material.

Each chapter takes humorous aim at a different aspect of Obamacare:

To get started **"Obamacare"** has a little of everything – some administration, some politics, some website, etc.

"Obamacare Website" focuses in on the disastrous development and launch of the Healthcare.gov website.

"Administrators, Staffers and Bureaucrats" takes a topsy turvy look at the Health and Human Services brain trust that should have made Obamacare work but didn't.

"Politics and Politicians" takes a jaded look at those denizens of the beltway and how they operate.

"Media" takes a look at the Fourth Estate who should have been alerting us to this impending disaster but didn't.

"Obamapourri" takes a closer look at the man at the top and the other people who have been running things with him.

There is even a bonus chapter, **"Obamacare Late Night"**, that features some of the best of the quips and one liners about Obamacare from news and the late night talk shows. And the index, **"Who's Who"**, tells you the characters used in the various jokes.

We hope everyone (maybe even some members of the Obama administration - although that may be a stretch :-) will enjoy this eclectic collection of humorous material and view it not as mean spirited but rather in the tradition of Jonathon Swift, Sinclair Lewis, *Mad Magazine*, *National Lampoon*, *the Onion*, late night comedians and other purveyors of humor, parody and satire.

◆ ◆ ◆

Publishers Note: We didn't write the Obamacare law - don't blame us!! It was having plenty of problems on its own long before we got here. If you don't think a bureaucratic quagmire of this magnitude is the least bit humorous in one sense we're in violent agreement with you. Millions of Americans are having their personal healthcare choices affected in major ways not anticipated when then Speaker of the House Nancy Pelosi famously told us, "But we have to pass the bill so that you can find out what is in it." And that's not funny.

On the other hand, love it or hate it, Obamacare is the law of the land and sometimes a little humor can make a point far better than a room full of politicians. And laughter, if not the best medicine, is certainly a good medicine. Take a look inside - we may not be able to make you forget all of the difficulties that Obamacare represents, but we may be able to convince you to at least smile at them a little.

◆ ◆ ◆

We hope you like the jokes. It was a lot of work to get this book out fast and if you do pass them on to your friends we would really appreciate it if you'd please mention that you saw them in our book. You can sign up for our newsletter to get more jokes at www.obamacarejokebook.com, you can "like" us on facebook at Obamacarejokes or follow us on our Twitter handle: @ObamacareJokes. Thank you!

◆ ◆ ◆

2.0   Obamacare

Q.   What is the official Obamacare motto?

A.   If at first you don't succeed, change the rules or grant an exemption.

◆ ◆ ◆

Advice from an Obama administration attorney to a member of the Obama administration staff about to testify about Obamacare before the House Committee on Oversight and Government Reform chaired by Republican Darrell Issa (R-CA): "You have the right to remain silent. Anything you say can and will be misquoted and then used against you."

◆ ◆ ◆

Q.   What do you get if you cross the 2,400+ page Obamacare law with the Godfather?

A.   An offer you can't understand.

◆ ◆ ◆

How about that major blunder at the U.S. Postal Service? They printed a stamp honoring President Obama and the launch of Obamacare only to discover that people were spitting on the wrong side!!

◆ ◆ ◆

President Obama held a closed door meeting with nervous executives from the insurance industry regarding the status of the ongoing Obamacare roll out. Later, he was asked "How did your meeting with the insurance industry executives go?" by Neil Cavuto of Fox Business News.

"Just fine," replied the satisfied President, "We had a very good discussion and a frank exchange of views. The insurance industry executives came in with their views and they left with mine."

◆ ◆ ◆

Q.   Why is Obamacare even better than eating an apple a day?

A.   With Obamacare the doctor stays away on his own.

◆ ◆ ◆

President Obama Announces Life Insurance Plan

Proposed law would require mandatory term life insurance for millions of uninsured Americans

Washington, D.C. -- Following up on the launch of the Patient Protection and Affordable Care Act (PPACA), popularly know as "Obamacare", the Obama administration today announced the Dead American and Affordable Funeral For You ("DAAFFY"). Already dubbed, "ObamaLife" by the press, if passed by Congress the new law would require mandatory term life insurance for all Americans.

"For far too long, many Americans have neglected to have any life insurance" stated President Obama in the White House Rose Garden where he was flanked by Senate Majority Leader Harry Reid, House Minority Leader Nancy Pelosi and a cadre of other senior Democrat law makers, "This leads to excessive financial strain on their families when they die. This proposed legislation will solve that problem for millions of uninsured Americans."

The proposed legislation would require all Americans over age 18 to have mandatory life insurance coverage. As with the PPACA, under the DAAFFY employers with over 50 full time employees would be required to provide life insurance to all employees or face a fine. Individuals not covered by employers and who do not already have life insurance would be required to purchase their own life insurance on exchanges modeled after the exchanges used by the PPACA. The new website, tentatively titled www.DeathSite.gov, would provide enrollees with a variety of life insurance purchasing options. For Americans purchasing life insurance on the exchanges premium subsidies would be available for individuals whose income was less than some arbitrarily large multiple of the federal poverty level.

"Now that we've learned about how to build a large, national insurance exchange this should be no sweat," continued President Obama. "After all, life insurance has a lot fewer variables to contend with than healthcare. We don't have all the details yet, but the Health and Human Services project management team thinks we can probably get this one built for under $350 million and we'll only need two years and 20-30 independent contractors - and this time we're going to try to use more American contractors."

One of the interesting aspects of the proposed legislation is the elimination of the pre-existing conditions requirements of most life insurance policies, particularly death. "Historically, refusing to issue life insurance to the sick and the dead has allowed greedy life insurance companies to profit unfairly in a highly discriminatory manner," continued the President. "This was inherently discriminatory and perhaps racial profiling since members of many minorities have shorter life expectancies. Under the proposed new law this discrimination would be banned and individuals or their families would be able to apply for life insurance coverage for up to three months after the death of an applicant without regard to pre-existing conditions."

Another unique aspect of the proposed DAAFFY law is that a portion of all life insurance proceeds would now be paid directly to the federal government upon the death of the policy holder. "We want to take the humane step of simplifying estate planning for individuals who are dealing with the grief and disruption brought about by the death of a loved one," explained the President.

Under the proposed DAAFFY legislation a percentage of all life insurance proceeds would now be remitted by the insurance companies directly to the Department of the Treasury upon the filing of any claim for death benefits. The exact amount would be on a sliding scale from 10% to 90% based upon the income and net worth of the deceased individual. The President continued, "I have instructed the IRS to prepare proposed regulations to enforce the new law and to collect the government's share of the insurance proceeds."

People who already have life insurance policies will be able to keep their life insurance under a grandfathering program modeled after that of the PPACA. "Let me be clear," said the President. "If you like your life insurance you can keep your life insurance. Period. And, if you are already dead, enrollment is optional."

However, under DAAFFY the proceeds of all life insurance policies, including that of grandfathered policies, would immediately become subject to the new tax provisions included in the proposed new law and, should any terms of the life insurance policy change, that policy will be cancelled and the policy holder will be required to enroll in a government approved life insurance policy. "We're going to eliminate many 'junk' life insurance polices which collect premiums for years then pay off only when the policy holder actually dies," continued Obama.

Senate Majority Leader Harry Reid (D-NV) said he expected prompt passage of DAAFFY in the Democrat controlled Senate. "For far too long life insurance companies have preyed on dead Americans," commented Reid. "DAAFFY will go a long ways toward correcting this injustice and let's face it, under the new Senate filibuster rules I can get 51 votes from Democrat Senators in safe seats to vote for DAAFFY or pretty much any other ridiculous entitlement program that we can come up with."

However, when asked for comments on the proposed legislation, Speaker of the House John Boehner (R-OH) appeared dubious. "I think the President may be getting a bit ahead of himself in proposing another huge new entitlement program fresh on the heels of Obamacare," commented Boehner, "We're going to be cleaning up that PPACA mess for quite a while and I don't think there is much appetite to be taking on any major new entitlement programs. I think it would be safe to say that the proposed DAAFFY mandatory life insurance law will probably be 'Dead On Arrival' in the House."

◆ ◆ ◆

Secret Obamacare Staff Skills Review Terms

Review Term	Secret Meaning
Good presentation skills	Can bullshit standing up
Good communication skills	Spends lots of time on phone
Well qualified	Married to a Democrat
Exceptionally well qualified	Married to a Democrat Senator
Work is first priority	Has no life
Socially active	Drinks a lot
Family is socially active	Spouse drinks a lot, too
Works well independently	Nobody knows what they do
Works well in the field	Never shows up in the office
Highly intelligent	Wears glasses
Agile intellect	Probably has A.D.D.
Quick thinking	Always has a good excuse
Flexible	Blames everybody else
Confrontational style	Punches co-workers
Very confrontational style	Punches supervisor
Highly focused	Does one thing at a time
Thoughtful	Sleeps at desk
Analytical	Can't make a decision
Careful	Won't make a decision
Assertive	Obnoxious
Aggressive	Very obnoxious
Delegates well	Gets someone else to do work
Good command of language	Speaks English
Attentive to details	Nit picker
Highly attentive to details	Anal retentive nit picker
Good leadership qualities	Intimidates others
Good judgment	Flips coin to makes decisions
Exceptionally good judgment	Agrees with Sebelius's decisions
Team player	Ass kisser
Strong team player	Exceptionally good ass kisser
Team leader	Unbelievably good ass kisser
Good sense of humor	Laughs at bosses jokes
Career minded	Back stabber
Loyal	Has not testified to Congress yet

◆ ◆ ◆

On the way to a conference to discuss Obamacare, Nobel Prize winning economist Paul Krugman, New York Mayor Michael Bloomberg and Vice President Joe Biden were sharing a ride when their limo was hit by a garbage truck and they were all killed. Upon arriving at the Pearly Gates, they were surprised to find themselves waiting in line with Federal Reserve Chairman Ben Bernanke who had died suddenly that same day. It looked like it was going to be a long wait in line, so to pass the time Bernanke suggested they all share a little bit about their lives before their untimely deaths.

Krugman replied first, saying that he had a PhD from MIT, had been an internationally known author and lecturer, had been a professor of economics at Princeton University, had won the Nobel Prize in economics in 2008 and that his IQ was over 160.

"Wonderful," said Bernanke, "We can discuss Obamacare, its effect on macroeconomics and its impact on the growth of the U.S. economy." Turning to Mayor Bloomberg, Bernanke asked, "How about you, Mr. Mayor?"

Mayor Bloomberg replied that his IQ was 135, that he had an MBA from Harvard, was a self made billionaire entrepreneur and now that his final term as Mayor of New York had ended he had been looking forward to returning to private sector venture capital to help develop more successful, socially conscious businesses.

"Excellent," said Bernanke, "We can discuss the impact that Obamacare will have on local governments and also how Obamacare will impact corporate healthcare expenditures and employee wellness." Finally, he turned to Vice President Biden and asked, "What about you, Mr. Vice President?"

Biden replied that he didn't know his IQ but he had a Law Degree from Syracuse University and before becoming Vice President he had served 36 years in the U.S. Senate.

"So," replied Bernanke after some thought, "How about those Nationals?"

◆ ◆ ◆

10 Things about Obamacare that President Obama will never admit in public:

10. Originally wanted to name the bill, "Now The Government Has You By The Balls" Act.

9. Might have underestimated people's negative reactions to losing their current insurance plans.

8. Might have <u>seriously</u> underestimated people's negative reactions to losing their family doctor.

7. Might have <u>really seriously</u> underestimated people's negative reactions to losing their job or having their hours reduced because their employer can't afford Obamacare.

6. Never had any intention of enrolling himself or his family in the program.

5. Actually believed you could cover 50 million uninsured and lower costs at the same time.

4. <u>Nobody</u> understands the health insurance business model.

3. Really didn't read the bill before he signed it.

2. Believed Kathleen Sebelius could manage a massive IT project.

1. Had his fingers crossed behind his back whenever he said, "If you like your insurance you can keep it. Period.".

◆ ◆ ◆

Before the website launched Obamacare teetered on the edge of the abyss. Since the launch it has taken great strides forward.

♦ ♦ ♦

Q.   What do you call an Obamacare navigator who can answer 20% of the new Obamacare enrollee's questions?

A.   An overachiever.

♦ ♦ ♦

Q.   What's the difference between a used car salesman and an Obamacare navigator explaining various insurance options under Obamacare?

A.   The used car salesman knows he's lying - and he can probably drive a car.

♦ ♦ ♦

An applicant was filling out the Health and Human Services job application to become an Obamacare navigator. Near the end of the application he came to the question, "Have you ever been arrested?" to which he answered, "No."

The next question, obviously intended only for people who had answered "Yes" to the "prior arrest" question, was "Why?" The applicant, not the sharpest knife in the drawer, answered it anyway: "Never been caught."

♦ ♦ ♦

After a few drinks at the Tombs in Georgetown, comedian Greg Gutfeld leans over to the big guy next to him at the bar and says, "Want to hear the latest Obamacare joke?"

The big guy glares at him and replies, "Well, friend, before you tell that joke you should know that I'm 6'1", 210 pounds, a former ACORN organizer and I work as an Obamacare navigator."

Before Gutfeld can say anything back, the even bigger guy next to the big guy says, "I'm 6'3", 230 pounds, a member of Occupy Wall Street and I'm an Obamacare navigator, too."

Finally, the huge guy down the bar next to the bigger guy says, "I'm 6'5", 260 pounds, a member of SEIU, worked for the Obama campaigns in both 2008 and 2012 and I now work at the Department of Health and Human Services as an Obamacare administrator."

The big guy now turns back to Gutfeld and says, "Now, buddy, do you really still want to tell that Obamacare joke?"

"No, I guess not," Gutfeld replies, "I'd really hate to have to explain it three times."

◆ ◆ ◆

Obamacare

(Parody lyrics sung to melody of traditional English ballad, "Scarborough Fair")

Have you signed up for Obamacare?
Forms, delays, poor choices and fines.
With high co-pays, expenses I share.
All this now for coverage of mine.

Signed up for silver, the premiums hurt.
Forms, delays, poor choices and fines.
Deductible's huge, will cost me my shirt.
Costs too much for coverage of mine.

Discovered my doctor's not on my plan.
Forms, delays, poor choices and fines.
He'll only treat me for cash in his hand,
Will not accept this coverage of mine.

Local hospitals signed: none altogether.
Forms, delays, poor choices and fines.
So if I need care I'll be paying forever.
Worthless is this coverage of mine.

Have you signed up for Obamacare?
Forms, delays, poor choices and fines.
Actually, fines are sounding much better.
They can stuff this coverage of mine.

◆ ◆ ◆

President Obama, director Steven Spielberg and Senator Ted Cruz (R-TX) are captured by cannibals on a remote Pacific island. Asked by the chief of the tribe for one last request before he has them boiled for dinner, Spielberg thinks for a moment then says, "I'd like to see a final screening of *Citizen Kane*, the greatest movie ever made."

The chief, while personally preferring *Eating Raoul*, agrees.

President Obama, when asked for his last request, responds, "I'd like to Skype one final speech back home to once again explain to all Americans how Obamacare is going to solve healthcare problems, bring insurance to the uninsured, improve coverage for those who already have insurance and lower healthcare costs across the land. Even though there have been some initial difficulties, I still consider this my crowning achievement and I know it will be remembered as my legacy forever."

Not sure what it all means, the chief nonetheless agrees, but before they can get the Skype hook up connected, Cruz blurts out his request: "For God's sake, please **BOIL ME NOW** so I won't have to listen to President Obama's speech."

◆ ◆ ◆

Given the mounting questions regarding Obamacare, the Iranian nuclear negotiations, Benghazi, Syria, the IRS investigations, NSA snooping, Fast and Furious gun running, et. al., here's one thought members of the Obama administration always keep in mind:

A bad memory is often better than a clear conscience.

◆ ◆ ◆

"Well," said one friend to another, "I've got good news and I've got bad news. The good news is that I finally succeeded in enrolling in Obamacare. The bad news is that I'm going to have to sell my car to pay the premiums."

◆ ◆ ◆

Obamacare Enrollee Haikus

My old insurance gone.
New policy, higher price.
How is this better?

Keeping my insurance
Is an option no longer.
This was not a lie?

Patience to enroll.
Your rage is of little worth.
The website is down.

Wait. And wait. And wait.
And still the website silent.
My butt growing sore.

Continue or not?
Website demands I respond.
Either way I lose.

Call to Obamacare
Enrollment answered at last.
I still hear laughter.

Data entered for
Enrollment gone without trace.
My screams go unheard.

At last I see the
Exchange insurance rates for me.
I am throwing up.

At last I'm enrolled.
But my doctor now has quit.
Horrors never end!

New coverage at
Last. Expensive. Limited
Answer: Don't get sick!

♦ ♦ ♦

10 Least Requested Insurance Coverages You Now Have Thanks To Obamacare

10. Hangnail transplant surgery

9. Bad aroma therapy

8. Two words: Butt liposuction

7. Haitian voodoo witch doctor visits

6. Bloodletting

5. Botox hemorrhoid treatments

4. Brazilian bikini waxing

3. Tapeworm diet

2. Leech therapy

1. Brazilian bikini waxing - for Men!

♦ ♦ ♦

How about that new McDonalds fast food value meal patterned after Obamacare? You just order anything you want from the menu and the person behind you has to pay for it.

◆ ◆ ◆

Many comedians think Obamacare is a great joke. Unfortunately, so do a lots of accountants, doctors, hospitals, insurance companies, people who already had healthcare insurance they liked, businesses and other Americans.

◆ ◆ ◆

Obamacare Law Cancels Federal Holidays

Washington, D.C. -- In a surprising discovery it was learned today that an obscure provision of the Patient Protection and Affordable Care Act that becomes effective in 2014 cancels all Federal holidays including New Year's Day, Martin Luther King Day, President's Day, Memorial Day, Independence Day, Labor Day, Columbus Day, Veteran's Day, Thanksgiving Day and Christmas Day. The law was passed in 2010 with exclusively Democrat votes.

"Well," said Speaker of the House John Boehner (R-OH), "The Democrats always said we had to read it to learn what's in it. Well, we're learning more every day. New taxes, cancelled insurance, more regulations, fewer doctors, higher costs and now all Federal holidays cancelled. I shudder to think what we'll find next."

Former Speaker of the House Nancy Pelosi (D-CA) commented, "Hey, I never read this provision either, but I know we never said, 'If you like your holiday you can keep it'."

When asked for a comment, White House Press Secretary Jay Carney said, "Federal holidays that met the new Federal holiday provisions included in the Affordable Care Act could have been grandfathered in but none of the current holidays met those requirements. If necessary, I'm sure that President Obama will consider issuing executive orders delaying the cancellation of selected holidays until after the 2014 mid-term elections."

◆ ◆ ◆

Rejected choices for the "official" Obamacare slogan:

10. Obamacare - The healthcare plan of yesterday, tomorrow.

9. Obamacare - You think you hate it now but wait until you try it.

8. Obamacare - Comprehensive coverage even a zombie could love.

7. Obamacare - Sure, it's not perfect today but just you wait.

6. Obamacare - It's not a tax, just a burden.

5. Obamacare - Learn it. Love it. Live it.

4. Obamacare - If it was better we wouldn't have exempted ourselves.

3. Obamacare - Coverage so good we had to force you to buy it.

2. Obamacare - You can't always get what you want - or what you need.

1. Obamacare - We <u>still</u> don't know what's in it.

◆ ◆ ◆

An attractive woman was confiding in one of her girl friends that even though she had been married three times her marriages had never been consummated.

"What about your first husband?" asked the amazed friend.

"Well, it turned out that he was gay so he wouldn't," replied the woman.

"And what about your second husband?" continued the friend.

"Well," said the friend, "He was badly injured in the Gulf war so he couldn't."

"And what about your current husband?" continued the bemused friend.

"Well, he's working on Obamacare at the Department of Health and Human Services," said the frustrated wife. "And if he gets home at all, all he can do is sit on the side of the bed and talk about how much better it will be than what I've had before and how insanely great it is going to be when I finally get it."

♦ ♦ ♦

Sebelius to Make Guest Appearance on Popular TV Show

Hollywood -- There's an unconfirmed rumor that on an upcoming episode of *Fear Factor* there will be a special segment where they lower Health and Human Services Secretary Kathleen Sebelius into a pit full of enraged voters whose insurance policies were cancelled and who lost their doctors because of Obamacare.

♦ ♦ ♦

Obamacare: It won't be hard to swallow. It's a suppository!

♦ ♦ ♦

Bumper sticker seen around the Health and Human Services Offices in Washington D.C.:

OBAMACARE: RESISTANCE IS FUTILE. YOU WILL BE ASSIMILATED.

♦ ♦ ♦

10 Rejected Names for Obamacare

10. The Insurance Administrators Employment Security Act

9. The Keep Your Insurance Plan If You Can Act

8. The We Know What Insurance Plan Is Really Best For You Act

7. The You Can Read It After It's Too Late Act

6. The Spend More To Get Less Insurance Coverage Act

5. The Higher Insurance Deductibles and Premiums Are In Your Future Act

4. The Doctor Availability Reduction and Restriction Act

3. The Congress Has Our Own Plan and The Rest Of You Are On Your Own Act

2. The Unimagined and Unintended Consequences Act

1. The Limited Choices and Unaffordable Care Act

◆ ◆ ◆

God, having reached the end of His patience with the human race, decides to send down His angels to destroy the earth. Wanting to give the people at least some opportunity to repent, He summons Pope Francis, former President George W. Bush and President Barack Obama and informs them that the world will end at precisely 12:01 AM, GMT, two weeks from this day of notice. As the three men begin to leave, God motions to President Obama to come closer and whispers something in his ear. After listening, Obama nods his head in understanding and then leaves to catch up with the others.

Pope Francis immediately returns to the Vatican and summons the College of Cardinals. "Well," says the Pope, "I've got some good news and some bad news. The good news is that we were right all along and there is, in fact, a God. The bad news is that He is really pissed off and the world is going to end at 12:01 AM, GMT, two weeks from today. Notify the faithful to repent and prepare."

Former President Bush immediately returns to his Texas ranch and summons Republican leaders. "Well," says W., "I've got some bad news and some good news. The bad news is that God is really pissed off and He is going to destroy the world at 12:01 AM, GMT, two weeks from today. The good news is that we won't have to listen to President Obama blaming us for everything any longer."

President Obama immediately returns to the White House, calls Congressional Democrats, his cabinet members and senior staff into an emergency meeting. "Well," says the President to the assembled officials, "I've got some really good news and some really bad news. God is really pissed off and He is going to destroy the world at 12:01 AM, GMT, two weeks from today. The really good news is that since He is going to destroy the world we're not going to have to worry about debugging Obamacare or going to any more of those stupid congressional hearings. The really bad news is that God told me personally that he knows that we lied repeatedly to the American people about Obamacare and **WE'RE ALL GOING TO HELL!**"

◆ ◆ ◆

10 Signs your Obamacare Navigator has completely lost it:

10. Responds, "Hah! Wouldn't you like to know?" to all questions.

9. Grabs your crotch to check if you're wearing a wire.

8. Keeps asking you if this is a test.

7. Asks if you'd like fries with that insurance.

6. Keeps muttering about "credible deniability."

5. Wants to know if you know of any job openings in the private sector.

4. Asks if you know a good attorney.

3. When calling on the phone you realize the drooling you keep hearing is not coming from a pet bulldog.

2. Insists you sign a non-disclosure agreement before he'll talk with you.

1. Tells you, "Sorry. I'd really, Really, REALLY like to help you enroll in Obamacare but the website is down again."

◆ ◆ ◆

The implementation of Obamacare has disrupted the financial plans of millions of families across the country. One couple's private insurance policy of many years was cancelled when Obamacare became the law and the replacement Obamacare coverage was going to be much more expensive. They sat down to go over their household budget to see what expense cuts they would need to make to balance their household budget to pay for the more expensive replacement insurance.

"My dear," said the husband, "If you'd just learn to get around better in the kitchen, we could do without the cook."

"My dear," retorted his wife, "If you'd just learn to get around better in the bedroom, we could do without the gardener."

◆ ◆ ◆

A guy walking along the beach finds a bottle floating in the surf and picks it up. When he pulls out the cork there is a bright flash, a puff of blue smoke and a genie who looks and sounds just like Gilbert Gottfried pops out of the bottle and says, "Thank you for releasing me. For your kindness, I will grant you one wish."

The guy says, "I've always wanted to visit Hawaii, but I can't because I'm terrified of flying and I get deathly seasick on ships. So my wish is for you to build a bridge from Los Angeles to Honolulu so that I can drive to Hawaii in my car."

The genie says, "I'm sorry, but I just don't think I can do that. The amount of work involved is unimaginable. Just think of all the cement and steel that would be needed to build the huge pilings and abutments required to hold up the bridge – they would need to reach thousands of feet down to the bottom of the Pacific Ocean. Plus, since a bridge from Los Angeles to Hawaii would be over 2,400 miles long, there would have to be gas stations, restaurants and rest stops all along the way. No, that is just too much to ask. You're just going to have to come up with another wish."

Disappointed, the guy thinks for a couple minutes then says, "Well, there is one other thing. I'm self-employed, my private family health insurance plan that we've had for years was cancelled because of the Affordable Care Act and I'm baffled by the whole process of how to sign up for insurance on the new exchanges. What coverages are available? What's the real cost going to be compared to my old insurance? How do I enroll my family? How can I compare the available plans? I'd really like some help in evaluating all my options to select the best replacement policy I can afford for me and my family. Please, explain Obamacare to me!!"

The genie thinks for a couple of seconds then replies, "OK, fine. So would that bridge to Hawaii be two lanes or four?"

◆ ◆ ◆

According to the Heritage Foundation, "Obamacare is a cancer".

WRONG! Obamacare was signed into law on March 23, 2010. That make it an Aries. The Obamacare website, Healthcare.gov, on the other hand, launched on October 1, 2013 making it a Libra. And, since Aries and Libra are opposed signs, they don't work very well together. No kidding!

◆ ◆ ◆

Nationalizing health insurance is not a new concept. Over 20 years ago, during the 1993 debate over Hillarycare, Hillary Clinton explained why Americans needed a national healthcare system to mandate our choices on healthcare spending:

"We just think people will be too focused on saving money and they won't get the care for their children and themselves that they need," said Mrs. Clinton. "The money has to go to the Federal Government because the Federal Government will spend that money better."

And with Obamacare, we're getting a chance to see first hand just how well that approach is working out.

◆ ◆ ◆

The Obama administration reported today that as a result of Obamacare eventually every American's healthcare costs will be lower. For most people, this is expected to occur sometime after they die.

◆ ◆ ◆

3.0   Obamacare Website

Q.   What's the difference between the Obamacare website launch and the Titanic?

A.   After sailing on its maiden voyage the Titanic stayed up for three days before it went down.

◆ ◆ ◆

Q.   What's the difference between an out of control airplane spiraling down toward the ground and more than a few Obamacare enrollees visiting the Healthcare.gov website?

A.   One results in a crash site, the other results in a site crash.

◆ ◆ ◆

A little girl asked her father, "Daddy, do all fairy tales begin with, 'Once upon a time'?"

"No Sweetie," replied Dad. "A lot of fairy tales begin with, 'Thank you for enrolling in Obamacare. Your satisfaction is very important to us...'."

◆ ◆ ◆

Q.   What is the definition of "multi-user" on Obamacare's Healthcare.gov website?

A.   When users from two or more states who are trying to enroll in Obamacare are staring at the same "Website currently busy and unavailable" message at the same time.

◆ ◆ ◆

Q.   How many Obamacare software developers does it take to write a web application with a simple, easy to follow, user-friendly front end and a clean, highly secure back end that can efficiently enroll millions of Americans in Obamacare?

A.   More

◆ ◆ ◆

10 ways things would be different if Jeff Bezos and Amazon had managed the development of the Healthcare.gov website:

10. No one would have to ask, "Who's in charge?"

9. The website would have been developed in six months, tested for a year before launch and cost less than $5 million to develop.

8. The website would be able to handle 10 zillion visitors simultaneously and follow up every one of them for years with daily email sales pitches for related products.

7. Project development status reports would not receive four Pinocchios from the *Washington Post.*

6. Democrats who voted for Obamacare would not be contemplating mass suicide.

5. Republicans who didn't vote for Obamacare would be contemplating mass suicide.

4. You'd be able to put your choice of healthcare plans, a ski parka, some CDs, a couple DVDs and a garden hose into your shopping cart and have them all delivered to your house in two days with free shipping.

3. For developers not meeting the project schedule, two words: <u>You're Fired</u>!

2. Congress would have lots more time to investigate the Benghazi, IRS, NSA and Fast and Furious scandals.

1. The website would actually <u>WORK</u>!!!

♦ ♦ ♦

Obamacare Website Roll Out Haikus

Time has come for me
To enroll in an exchange.
I am not enthused.

Obamacare website
Unavailable. Says to
Return tomorrow

TV still reports
Healthcare.gov sucking big time.
This is not good news.

Website updated.
More bugs than before were found.
Not a big surprise.

Data base crash leaves
few options available.
My foreboding grows.

Exchanges still down.
My hope fades to a glimmer.
I fear repeal looms.

Site hackers are said
To have more success than we.
If true, we're so screwed!

◆ ◆ ◆

A male software engineer working on the Obamacare website
was taking a walk one day when, to his surprise, he heard a frog
call out to him from a shrub and say, "If you kiss me, I'll turn
into a beautiful princess."

Intrigued, he bent over, picked up the frog, put it in his pocket
and continued on his walk. After a while, the frog spoke up again
and said, "If you kiss me, I'll turn back into a princess. I'm 19,
I'm beautiful and I'll be your girl friend for the next month." The

programmer took the frog out of his pocket, smiled, stroked it lovingly and gently returned it to his pocket.

Still later, the frog spoke up again, "Look, if you kiss me, I'll turn back into a princess. I'm 19, I'm beautiful, I'm incredibly sexy, I'll be your love slave for a year and I'll do anything - and I mean ANYTHING - you want." Again the programmer took the frog out, smiled, stroked it lovingly and gently returned it to his pocket.

Finally, the frustrated frog screamed, "DUDE, WHAT IS YOUR PROBLEM? I've told you I'm a beautiful, sexy princess. I've told you that I'll stay with you for a year. I've told you that I'll be your love slave and do anything you want. Why won't you kiss me?"

Finally, the programmer took the frog out, gazed into its eyes and said, "Look, I'm working on the data base interfaces for the Obamacare website. The software is impossibly complicated because we have to interface to dozens of government and insurance industry legacy data bases to get all of the applicant information this stupid law requires so that we can complete the application process. We're going to be busy for years trying to make this WOMBAT* work correctly and there is no way I'm going to have any time available for a girlfriend, let alone a love slave. But having a talking frog is, like, really cool."

*WOMBAT: Geek speak for "Waste Of Money, Brains And Time"

♦ ♦ ♦

Q. All the senior members of the Obamacare website development team are in a rapidly sinking boat. Who gets saved?

A. America's healthcare system.

♦ ♦ ♦

Q. What's the difference between the Obamacare website and a car battery?

A. The car battery has a positive side.

♦ ♦ ♦

10 Lines from Congressional hearings on the Obamacare website launch that indicated there were BIG problems:

10. "What do you expect? We only had over three years and $600+ million to develop the website!"

9. "My lawyer wouldn't want me to answer that question."

8. "Calling '911' didn't help."

7. "I'm sorry but we've been instructed to play dumb."

6. "At least people can still get useful medical information on WebMD.com for free."

5. "We thought 'scalable architecture' had something to do with getting bigger offices for Obamacare staff."

4. "Uhhh ... maybe you should call one of the enrollment navigators to answer that."

3. "I'll call you back later if I find out anything."

2. "Nobody mentioned to us that people could keep their policies if they liked them."

1. "You'll have to enroll in it to know what's in it."

♦ ♦ ♦

We understand that there is no truth to the rumor that an Obamacare enrollee who tried to use "penis" as his Healthcare.gov exchange login password had it rejected as, "Too Short".

♦ ♦ ♦

An Obamacare website software developer dies and upon arriving at the Pearly Gates is informed by Saint Peter that he must spend 10 years in purgatory before he will be allowed into Heaven. However, he does get to choose between software developer purgatory and Health and Human Services staff purgatory.

"What's the difference?" asked the curious software developer.

"Well," replied Saint Peter, "In software developer purgatory each day demons tie you to a stake, soak you in gasoline, light you on fire with a match and you burn for the next 12 hours. Then you get to rest for 12 hours. In HHS staff purgatory you wait around for 12 hours while the software developers burn then the demons tie you to a stake, soak you in gasoline, light you on fire with a match and you burn for the next 12 hours."

"Doesn't sound like much of a difference," said the software developer.

"If I were you," counseled Saint Peter, "I'd take HHS staff purgatory. The demons always show up late, the knots untie easily, the ropes tend to break, the stake is easy to pull out of the ground and somebody usually forgets the gasoline or the matches."

♦ ♦ ♦

Q.   How many Obamacare website project managers does it take to change a light bulb?

A.   None. Obamacare website project managers are perpetually in the dark.

♦ ♦ ♦

Ten Areas of Improvement for the Obamacare Website

10. Not need a national advertising campaign to convince people to use it

9. Have a landing page that doesn't have that soft pastel look of a feminine hygiene product website

8. Not need to recommend people call a toll free number or send in a paper application instead of enrolling online

7. Enrollee website enrollment would be faster than sending a paper application by carrier pigeon

6. Eliminate the "We're sorry but it's really busy right now. Why don't you try again when traffic is lighter - say around 3 AM" bounce pages

5. Provide premium and subsidy estimates more accurate than, "Well, now don't hold us to this but..."

4. Not automatically post enrollee's personal information to their Facebook wall

3. Eliminate eBay style bidding for an opportunity to enroll

2. Be able to actually sell the insurance policies people want to sign up for.

1. Actually look remotely like it might be worth the $600+ million and 3+ years it took to develop it

◆ ◆ ◆

A balloonist was up on a cross-country flight across southern Virginia. Unfortunately, the wind veered, blew him off course and forced him to land in an open field with no idea of where he was. Fortunately, a car was coming down a nearby road and he flagged it down. The balloonist asked the driver, "Can you please tell me where I am?"

"Yes, of course," said the driver. "You have just landed in the south field of Ayrshire Farm in Upperville, Virginia. The ranch is over 800 acres in total size with a variety of poultry and livestock. Also, there is a very aggressive Scottish Highland bull in the field and he is charging at you RIGHT NOW!!"

Just at that moment the bull lunged and flipped the balloonist over the fence. Fortunately, while a little banged up, he was not seriously hurt. As he got up and dusted himself off, he asked the driver, "So, how long did you work on the Obamacare website?"

"That's amazing!!" said the driver, taken aback, "You're spot on! I worked on the development of the Obamacare website from the beginning. How did you know that?"

"I've had to deal with Obamacare website developers many times," replied the balloonist. "The information you gave me was detailed, precise and accurate. Most of it was useless or redundant and by the time you got to the critical information I really needed it was almost too late to be of any help."

"So, how long did YOU work in the Obama administration?" retorted the driver.

Now it was the balloonist's turn to be surprised. "Unbelievable!! I was a deputy secretary in the Department of Health and Human Services. How could you possibly know that?"

"Because you didn't know where you were going, you still don't know where you are and you expect me to be able to help! So, you're just as lost as you were before we met, but now you think it's all my fault!"

◆ ◆ ◆

An Obamacare website developer became severely depressed and lost all interest in sex after the disastrous website roll out. His wife went to the doctor to get help in reviving her man's sex drive. "What about trying Viagra?" asked the doctor.

"No way," replied the distraught wife. "I can't even get him to take an aspirin for his constant headaches."

"No problem.", replied the doctor. "Just grind the pill into powder and put it into his coffee; he won't even taste it. Try it and come back in a week to let me know how it worked."

A week later the wife returned and the doctor inquired as to the results. "Oh, it was horrible, just horrible, doctor," cried the wife, bursting into tears.

"What happened?" asked the doctor.

"Well, I did just as you advised," she replied. "I ground up the pill and slipped the powder into his coffee. After about ten minutes the effect was amazing. He jumped up from his chair, swept everything off the table onto the floor, ripped my clothes off and then proceeded to make mad, passionate love to me right there on the tabletop. It was terrible!!"

"What was so terrible about that?" said the now confused doctor. "I thought you wanted a more exciting sex life."

"Oh, no doctor, please don't misunderstand!" said the mortified wife. "The sex was the best we've had in 15 years, but I'll never be able to show my face at that Applebee's restaurant again."

♦ ♦ ♦

If the Health and Human Services Department team that managed the Obamacare website development had been running the Sahara desert it would have run out of sand.

♦ ♦ ♦

Q.   What do you need when you have the Obamacare website development team up to their necks in concrete?

A.   More concrete.

◆ ◆ ◆

Five Stages of Grief For Obamacare Website Developers

Denial   Everything is almost working. Really. It's just like any other large IT project. Just a few minor issues to fix. We'll have all the bugs worked out shortly and have it completely running very soon. Just trust us.

Anger   Those miserable Republicans and all those greedy insurance companies are behind all of this bad press coverage. And they never even wanted it to work anyway. We'll show them!

Bargaining   If you'll just give us six more months and a few hundred million more dollars we know we could make it all work just fine. Really. Please. PLEASE!!

Depression   We're never going to finish. This thing is so loaded with bugs and design flaws that it will never run correctly. What were we thinking, trying something this ambitious?

Acceptance   Sigh! Oh well, who cares if we ever finish this turkey? It's not like Obamacare was ever going to be that popular anyway.

◆ ◆ ◆

Who says the government never does anything as efficiently as the private sector? The design of the Healthcare.gov website with it's many interconnections between numerous government, healthcare and insurance company data bases provides a veritible "one stop" shopping mall for hackers and identity thieves!

◆ ◆ ◆

4.0   Administrators, Staffers and Bureaucrats

Q.   How many Obamacare administrators at the Department of Health and Human Services does it take to change a light bulb?

A.   Thirty-five. Five to form a committee to determine if the bulb really needs to be changed, three to prepare the bid proposal for vendors to submit to supply the replacement bulb, five to verify all potential bulb vendors comply with OSHA, ERISA, ADA and all other applicable regulations, five to perform an environmental impact study, one to award the contract to supply the replacement bulb to the winning vendor, one to supervise the vendor actually changing the bulb, five to write the final report to Congress and ten to complete the Paperwork Reduction Act paperwork.

◆ ◆ ◆

Q.   How do you keep an Obamacare administrator from drowning?

A.   Shoot him before he hits the water.

◆ ◆ ◆

Q.   What's the difference between the Department of Health and Human Services Obamacare enrollment projections and vivid sexual fantasies?

A.   The sexual fantasies are based upon things that you can actually imagine.

◆ ◆ ◆

One way that Obamacare insurance providers are trying to keep costs down is by using so called "Skinny Networks" that have a very limited number of physicians available to patients in their healthcare plans. You know you're in big trouble when you sign up for Obamacare and discover that the only doctor in your selected healthcare plan's "Skinny Network" is Dr. Kevorkian.

◆ ◆ ◆

Secret Guide to Obamacare Internal Memos

What They Say	What It Means
I'm looking at a number of different approaches.	I have no clue what to do at this point.
Closer project coordination.	Let's get together for lunch.
We're forming a consensus.	Nobody agrees with anybody on this.
Let's compare notes.	Maybe I can steal an idea from you.
We need to flesh this out more.	Not nearly enough bullshit yet.
I have to push back on that.	Probably the dumbest idea I've ever heard.
I'm having an extensive report prepared on a fresh approach.	Maybe the private sector has a clue on how to fix this mess.
The entire concept has to be abandoned.	Even I couldn't get this one past the Congressional Budget Office.
It is "in process".	Major politics involved; no chance it will ever happen.
I will look into it.	Forget it! I already have too many problems.
Please keep me in the loop.	It's your problem, now!

What They Say	What It Means
Please note and initial.	I'm spreading the responsibility for this around.
Give me your interpretation.	I can't wait to hear how you spin this to Congress.
We need input from the top.	No way am I getting thrown under the bus for this disaster.
We need input from the staff.	They feel better when they think we listened to them.
Give me the benefit of your thinking.	I'll listen as long as you agree with me.
Let's schedule a conference call for the whole team.	I could use a nap.
Let's discuss in person.	I screwed up.
See me.	Come to my office, I really screwed up.
I'm following our standards.	That's the way I have always done it.
Text me the data.	I'm too lazy to write it down.
I didn't get your e-mail.	I didn't look. I haven't checked my e-mail for days.

◆ ◆ ◆

Q. What's the best thing to throw an Obamacare administrator sinking in quicksand?

A. An anvil.

♦ ♦ ♦

Q. What's the definition of *ambivalence?*

A. An Obamacare administrator driving off a cliff in your new Tesla Model S.

♦ ♦ ♦

Q. What do you call 25 skydiving Obamacare administrators falling through the sky?

A. Skeet. Or at least a "target rich" environment.

♦ ♦ ♦

Q. Why do they bury Obamacare senior administrators at least 20 feet under ground?

A. Deep down they are really good people.

♦ ♦ ♦

A former Obamacare administrator died in poverty and his former colleagues at Health and Human Services fanned out around Washington D.C. to raise funds for his funeral.

Upon arriving at the office of Senate Minority Leader Mitch McConnell (R-KY) they asked that he donate a dollar for the administrator's funeral. "Only one dollar?" asked McConnell, "Only one dollar to bury an Obamacare Administrator? Here's my check; go bury 5,000 more of them."

♦ ♦ ♦

Healthcare.gov signups discovered,
Website bugs and malfunctions uncovered.
But slowness to fix it
Caused enrollees to nix it
And Obamacare never recovered

♦ ♦ ♦

Obamacare Administrator Haikus

Republicans have
Offered some more ideas.
Like, as if we care.

Enrollees expect
site to sell them insurance now.
What silly lemmings.

Loss of family
Doctor could be a plus. Your
Horizons expand.

You keeping your plan
Or doctor wasn't our plan.
Tough. Get over it.

Insurance exchanges
Too complex to understand.
It's a house of cards.

Spending more for your
Healthcare is good. Clarify
Your priorities.

New York Times always
reports Obamacare is great.
Reporters love us!

Enrollment numbers
Not close to meeting our goals.
Need a good story.

Enrollment numbers
Remaining far, far too low.
Need better story.

Enrollment numbers
Are never going to work.
We're totally screwed.

♦ ♦ ♦

Ms. Sebelius

(Parody lyrics sung to melody of "Mrs. Robinson", by Paul Simon)

And here's to you, Ms. Sebelius.
Barack loves you more than you will know.
Whoa! Whoa! Whoa!

God bless you please, Ms. Sebelius.
Website's down so no more time to play!
Hey! Hey! Hey!
Hey! Hey! Hey!

We'd like to have more details
How you built it
For our files.
We'd like to have you
Tell us who you paid.
Look around you. All you see
Are press and TV guys.
Take the fifth unless
You want to go to jail.

And here's to you, Ms. Sebelius.
Barack loves you more than you will know.
Whoa! Whoa! Whoa!

God bless you, please, Ms. Sebelius.
Website's down so no more time to play!
Hey! Hey! Hey!
Hey! Hey! Hey!

Hide it in a spending bill
Where no one ever looks.
Pay fifty-five contractors for the project.
It's a little secret,
Just a CMS affair.
Most of all you've got to hide it
From the press.

Coo coo Ca-cho, Ms. Sebelius.
Barack loves you more than you will know.
Whoa! Whoa! Whoa!

God bless you, please, Ms. Sebelius.
Website's down so no more time to play!
Hey! Hey! Hey!
Hey! Hey! Hey!

Sitting on a slush fund
Full of cash and other perks.
Sending it to Canada in crates.
Database or
XML,
You lack any clues.
Every time the site goes down you lose.

Where have you gone, nervous Democrats?
The voters now are looking straight at you.
Woo! Woo! Woo!

What's that you say, Ms. Sebelius?
"Democrats have cut and run away."
Hey! Hey! Hey!
Hey! Hey! Hey!

◆ ◆ ◆

To liven up their working relationship, the Department of Health and Human Services Obamacare administration staff challenged the Obamacare website development team to a rowing race on the Potomac river running through Washington D.C. Agreeing on a 2,000 meter course using eight man racing sculls, both teams practiced hard and by race day they were as ready as they could be. Unfortunately, to the chagrin of the HHS staff, the software developers won easily by a solid 200 meters.

Afterwards, the HHS staff team was very depressed and they decided that the reason for their crushing defeat had to be found. After much discussion, a consulting group was hired and a working group from public relations, human resources, project management and finance was set up to investigate and report back. Committees were formed. No expense was spared. After three months of intense research and investigation the work group came up with the answer and the work group coordinator presented the summary to the assembled HHS senior administrators.

"To be brief," he said, "The problem was that the software developers had eight people rowing and one person steering. We here at HHS, on the other hand, had one person rowing and eight people steering."

Excited that the problem was now understood, the work group was asked to go away and come up with a plan so that HHS could win the following year's race and assuage their damaged pride. Two months later, the work group had developed a detailed plan for victory and the coordinator gave his short summary to the excited HHS staffers:

"Basically, that one person actually doing the rowing has got to row a lot harder."

◆ ◆ ◆

I've just visited the Healthcare.gov website for the first time.

I'm impressed.

I've never seen the phrase, "The Website is Currently Down for Maintenance and Unavailable. Please Check Back Later." presented on such a clear, colorful and user friendly screen.

◆ ◆ ◆

We hear that Health and Human Services was using Obamacare to test out their new microwave administrators. They spend 45 minutes working on the project and get paid for the whole day.

◆ ◆ ◆

Health and Human Services administration staff perspective on testifying about Obamacare before Congress:

Better to remain silent and appear clueless than to open your mouth and remove all doubt.

◆ ◆ ◆

10 Top Obamacare Administrator's Excuses for Why the Healthcare.gov Website Doesn't Work:

10. "The dog ate the analysis that projected how many people would actually sign up."

9. "Don't blame me – I was working with the IRS on enforcement."

8. "Bad Karma."

7. "Accidentally computed projected insurance subsidies for the exchanges in pesos."

6. "We think the Republicans had a gypsy curse placed on the website."

5. "There was not enough time for the project."

4. "There was enough time for the project but we spent it all in review meetings."

3. "Those Canadian contractors would never return our phone calls"

2. "We kept saying it wouldn't work but nobody in the White House would listen to us."

1. "It was all Bush's fault. (Hey, everyone else uses that, so why not us?)"

◆ ◆ ◆

A lowly Health and Human Services administrator was sitting in his office late one night when the Devil appeared before him. The Devil told the administrator, "I have a proposition for you. You can have job security for the rest of your life. You will be able to propose a set of comprehensive changes to fix Obamacare and they will sail through Congress and be approved with wide bipartisan support. The HHS Secretary will adore you and other members of the staff will be in awe of you."

The Devil continued, "In the next administration you will rise to become the Secretary of Health and Human Services yourself. The President will depend on you completely and when your term is over you will become a lobbyist and make obscene amounts of money. All I want in exchange is your soul, your wife's soul, your children's souls and the souls of your parents, grandparents and parents-in-law."

The staffer thought about this for a moment and then asked, "So, what's the downside?"

♦ ♦ ♦

What is the difference between realists, idealists and Health and Human Services Obamacare administrators?

Realists, when given a difficult problem, work because they know that if they succeed they will be rewarded and if they fail they will be punished.

Idealists, when given a difficult problem, work because they believe the solution may be good for mankind and that's reward enough for them.

Obamacare administrators, when given a difficult problem, work because 1) they know they'll get paid no matter what they do, 2) the final report will be late and make whatever solution they did come up with so complex and so confusing that no one will understand it anyway and 3) they can always blame everything on the Bush administration.

♦ ♦ ♦

THE FIVE RULES OF OBAMACARE ADMINISTRATION

1.　　**DON'T THINK**

2.　　If you think: **DON'T SPEAK.**

3.　　If you think and speak: **DON'T WRITE.**

4.　　If you think, write and speak: **DON'T TESTIFY.**

5.　　If you think, write, speak and testify:

DON'T BE SURPRISED AT WHAT HAPPENS!!

♦ ♦ ♦

Q.　　What's a good weight for an Obamacare administrator?

A.　　About 12 pounds, including the urn.

♦ ♦ ♦

ObamaCard

Develop Healthcare.gov website:	$	600,000,000
Obamacare insurance premium subsidies:	$	478,000,000,000
Take over U.S. healthcare:		$2,700,000,000,000
Cripple the U.S. economy for generations:		**PRICELESS**

There are some things in life that money can't buy. For everything else there's ObamaCard*, the official credit card for Obamacare and everything else in the ever expanding nanny state.

*ObamaCard is issued by the Bank of China. Offer may be withdrawn, modified or revoked at any time without notice.

♦ ♦ ♦

A visitor to an island inhabited by cannibals enters a village where there are a number of butcher shops, each specializing in a specific human organ. He stops at one shop which specializes in human brains from various government officials.

The brains are neatly arranged in a meat case and priced "by donor" according to a price list on the shop wall:

Federal Reserve trustee brains	$12/lb.
Wall Street lobbyist brains	$15/lb.
Senator brains	$18/lb.
Representative brains	$18/lb.
Obama executive czar brains	$110/lb.
Obamacare administrator brains	$150/lb.

Upon reading the prices, the traveler asked, "What makes the brains of Obama executive czars Obamacare administrators so expensive?"

"Are you kidding?" replied the cannibal, "Do you have any idea how hard it is to trap enough Obama executive czars and Obamacare administrators to get a pound of brains?"

"By the way," asked the traveler, "Does anybody around here have any Obama administration Department of Justice lawyer's brains?"

"No. Nobody is willing to clean them!" replied the cannibal.

◆ ◆ ◆

Sign on a Health and Human Services administrator's office wall:

If at first you don't succeed,
Destroy all evidence that you tried.

◆ ◆ ◆

It's a beautiful sunny day. You're by the pool. An Obamacare software developer and a senior Health and Human Services Obamacare administrator are both drowning and you can only save one of them. Do you go to lunch or read the paper?

◆ ◆ ◆

New Obamacare Healthcare Plans and Regulations Announced

Washington, D.C. -- Based on overwhelming consumer demand, Obamacare has added several new plan options. Joining the now familiar Bronze, Silver, Gold and Platinum plans are the new

Paper, Wood, Brick and Tin economy plans and the new Diamond super premium plan.

"These new Obamacare healthcare plans are intended to give enrollees even more options," said Health and Human Services Secretary Kathleen Sebelius. "The new economy plans are patterned after the popular cancelled 'junk insurance' plans that many Americans wanted to keep, offering coverage ranging from the super high deductible, lowest cost 'Paper' plan that is literally not worth the paper it's printed on up to the only ridiculous deductible 'Tin' plan. We've also added a new super premium 'Diamond' plan for people who basically want everything paid for by their healthcare insurance policy and can afford to pay through the nose for that kind of comprehensive coverage."

In a related story, HHS is issuing additional new regulations which require that all U.S. citizens must now be tissue typed. Mandated in another section of the PPACA act that nobody read, these regulations also make organ donation mandatory for all citizens. The new regulations will make arranging organ transplants much more efficient for high end policy holders. "For example," explained Sebelius, "With most insurance plans if you need an organ transplant you must either find a volunteer organ donor or go on the UNOS (United Network for Organ Sharing) priority list on a need ranked basis. However, with the new Diamond super premium plan if, for example, you need a heart transplant you go right to the head of the UNOS list and if no tissue matched heart is immediately available now we can hunt down and kill an uninsured person with the correct tissue match so you can get your new heart right away. After all, this kills two birds with one stone: it gets a premium paying Obamacare enrollee their new organ and at the same time gets one more 'free rider' out of the healthcare system."

◆ ◆ ◆

Two Obamacare administrators were walking back to their offices after lunch.

First Administrator, "I just got the most recent status update on the Healthcare.gov website and there's good news and bad news."

Second Administrator, "What's the good news?"

First Administrator, "Website performance is getting better by the day, we're having fewer crashes and we're scaling up to process more and more Obamacare enrollment applications every day."

Second Administrator, "So, what's the bad news?"

First Administrator, "Well, when the website was crashing all the time people couldn't stay online long enough to get information about their Obamacare options. Now that the website is working better, people are seeing the actual costs of signing up - the high premiums, the high deductibles, the limitations on physician networks, the limitations on hospitals, the reductions in prescription drug coverage, etc. Now they're REALLY pissed off."

♦ ♦ ♦

Now I lay me down to sleep,
I pray the Lord my soul to keep,
If I should die before I wake
**I HOPE IT'S NOT BECAUSE SOME
STUPID OBAMACARE NAVIGATOR
SCREWED UP MY FAMILY'S HEALTH
INSURANCE APPLICATION AFTER OUR
EXISTING INSURANCE POLICY WAS
CANCELLED BECAUSE OF OBAMACARE!**

♦ ♦ ♦

Bumper sticker seen around the Health and Human Services Offices in Washington D.C.:

**OBAMACARE. YOU THINK YOU HATE IT NOW BUT
WAIT UNTIL YOU'RE ENROLLED IN IT.**

♦ ♦ ♦

Q. How many people work on Obamacare at the Department of Health and Human Services?

A. Less than half.

♦ ♦ ♦

5.0   Politics and Politicians

A heated exchange between Republican Senator Ted Cruz (R-TX), a former prosecutor, and an Obamacare administrator during a Senate Finance Committee hearing on Obamacare:

Senator Cruz: "Did you conspire with other members of the Obama administration to defraud and deceive the public about Obamacare?"

Obamacare administrator: "No, Senator, I absolutely did not."

Senator Cruz: "You are aware that you are under oath?"

Obamacare administrator: "Yes, I am, Senator."

Senator Cruz: "And you are aware of the penalties for perjury?"

Obamacare administrator: "Yes, I am, Senator, and they're a hell of a lot less than the penalties for conspiracy and fraud."

◆ ◆ ◆

Republicans, Democrats in Rare Bi-Partisan Agreement

Washington, D.C. -- In a rare display of bi-partisan unanimity, the U.S. House of Representatives and the U.S. Senate have delayed the start of their various investigations into Obamacare until they have confirmed that all money budgeted by health insurance industry lobbyists for political contributions has, in fact, been distributed to all of the intended recipients.

◆ ◆ ◆

99 percent of politicians give the rest a bad name.

◆ ◆ ◆

The new insurance industry lobbyist slunk into the Congressman's office, looked furtively around and then pulled an envelope bulging with cash from his briefcase.

"Here's a $50,000 cash contribution," he said to the Congressman. "My client really needs your support for the Obamacare bill!"

The Congressman was outraged. "What kind of a corrupt Congressman do you think I am?" he asked, angrily, his face contorted and turning a mottled purple.

The lobbyist sputtered, embarrassed. "I ... I heard that we could 'work with you' and that we'd done it before!"

That calmed the Congressman down a little bit. "Look, son," he said, "Were I to accept your contribution now it would be a gross ethical transgression!"

"Why? What makes it unethical now?" said the lobbyist. "It's not like you haven't taken contributions from the insurance industry before."

The Congressman looked puzzled for a moment then smiled. "I don't think you understand. Business opponents of Obamacare have already contributed very handsomely for me to vote against this bill. Were I to take your money now it would present me with an irresolvable conflict of interest – why, I'd have to abstain!"

◆ ◆ ◆

NEWS BULLETIN: TERRORISTS SEIZE POLITICIANS

Washington, D.C. -- We have been unable to confirm that a group of Al-Qaeda terrorists has hijacked an airliner full of Senators and Representatives at Ronald Reagan National Airport and threatened to start releasing one politician every hour until their demands are met.

◆ ◆ ◆

A Democrat junior member of the House of Representatives was running for re-election and at a town hall meeting was under sharp attack by his Republican opponent for his support of Obamacare.

"My opponent has repeatedly called me a liar for telling you that under Obamacare if you liked your insurance you could keep it," said the embattled incumbent. "Rest assured that I never lied to you. It's just that the facts didn't quite match up with what I said."

◆ ◆ ◆

10 Public Statements About Obamacare that Senators and Representatives wish they had back (these are real!)

In politics success has many parents but failure is an orphan. However, as President Obama goes down with the ship over breaking his, "If you like your health plan you can keep it. Period." promise remember that he had lots and lots of help. Here are some similar quotes - five from Senators and five from members of the House of Representatives - who made the same promises as the President and there are HUNDREDS more just like these:

1. "This bill does not replace employer-sponsored coverage, it actually adds to the choices people have. If people like their insurance, they can keep it." Rep. John Lewis (D-GA)

2. "Again, if you like what you have, you will be able to keep it. Let me say this again: If you like what you have, when our legislation is passed and signed by the President, you will be able to keep it." - Sen. Patti Murray (D-WA)

3. "If you like the insurance you have, you can keep it. Don't listen to that stuff you heard in the last hour, Mr. Speaker. The truth is, you get to keep your health insurance if that's what you want." - Rep. Keith Ellison (D - MN)

4. "If you like the insurance that you have, you'll be able to keep it." - Sen. Mary Landrieu (D-LA)

5. "Let me be clear: if you like your current plan, you'll be able to keep it. Rather, we will build on our current system, so we can give you the freedom to choose what works best for you and your family. If you like your doctor, keep your doctor. If you like your current plan, keep your current plan." - Rep. Debbie Wasserman Schultz (D-FL)

6.　"We should begin with a basic principle: if you have coverage and you like it, you can keep it. If you have your doctor, and you like him or her, you should be able to keep them as well. We will not take that choice away from you." - Sen. Michael Bennet (D-CO)

7.　"Your premiums and other costs will not increase as a result of health care reform and if you like the coverage you have now, you'll be able to keep it. In fact, you'll get some additional help paying for premiums and out-of-pocket costs." Rep. John Conyers (D-NY)

8.　"Our bill says if you have health insurance and you like it, you can keep it" - Sen. Sherrod Brown (D-OH)

9.　"We need to build upon the current system of employer sponsored care, with a system that provides patients their choice of insurance coverage and their choice of doctors. In other words, if you like what you have, you should be able to keep it." Rep. Steny Hoyer (D-MD)

10.　"In fact, one of our core principles is that if you like the health care you have, you can keep it." - Sen. Harry Reid (D-NV)

♦ ♦ ♦

Obamacare promised the masses
Policies cheap for all classes
But when details emerged
Opposition, it surged
And supporters are now taking passes

♦ ♦ ♦

Q.　What's do you get when you cross the efficiency of the Health and Human Services administration with the gentle touch of the TSA and the compassion of the IRS?

A.　Obamacare.

♦ ♦ ♦

Taking a break from the highly partisan Obamacare hearings Senator Charles Schumer (D-NY) was browsing in a Washington D.C. antique shop and noticed a large sculpture on the back of one shelf. Reaching back, he found that it was a large, wonderfully detailed brass casting of a rat. "What a great paper weight," Schumer thought to himself. After haggling with the shop keeper over the price, he finally purchased the sculpture and left.

As he headed down the street, he thought he heard squeaking and scurrying noises behind him. He looked around and was astounded to see hoards of rats pouring out of the streets and alleys and heading straight for him. Panicking, he ran down the street with the ever increasing giant pack of rats in hot pursuit. The street ended at the edge of the Potomac River. Exhausted, Schumer ran to the very end of the pavement and, with all his strength, hurled the brass rat as far out into the river as he could. Amazingly, the rats scurried around him and leapt into the water where they all drowned. After breathing a huge sigh of relief and resting for a few minutes, Schumer headed back into the curio shop.

"Do you want to buy another brass rat?" asked the shop keeper.

"Forget the brass rats," said Schumer, "Do you have any brass Republicans?"

◆ ◆ ◆

At the height of a Congressional hearing on the Obamacare rollout disaster, Senator Elizabeth Warren (D-MA) attacked the insurance industry lobbyist testifying before the committee. "Isn't it true," asked the Senator, "That the votes of numerous Senators and members of the House of Representatives were influenced by insurance industry political contributions?"

The witness just sat there staring out into space, as though he had not heard the question. "Isn't it true that vast political influence for Obamacare in both the House and Senate was purchased with insurance industry money?" Warren repeated.

Still, the witness did not respond. Finally, the Chairman of the committee leaned forward and said, "The witness is directed to answer the Senator's question."

"Oh," replied the startled witness said, "I'm sorry. I thought she was addressing the other *members* of the committee."

◆ ◆ ◆

House Announces Rules for Scoring Obamacare Testimony

Washington, D.C. -- The United States House of Representatives today announced its new rules for scoring witnesses testifying before the various House Committees investigating Obamacare. This is a new approach for the House which has traditionally relied on shouting, long-winded questions and the ability to turn the witness' microphone on and off to score points during testimony.

"There has been a lot commentary regarding these hearings," said Speaker of the House John Boehner, (R-OH), "To the effect that the only reason we're having them is political posturing. Nothing could be further from the truth, and our new objective scoring system is going to prove that. We're going to ask hard questions and witnesses had better have good answers."

Under the new scoring system, patterned on the Olympics, all questions will be scored on difficulty and all responses will be scored on substance by an independent panel of seven international judges. The high and low scores will be eliminated and the five remaining scores averaged to produce the final score. The highest score would be 6.0 on both difficulty and substance. Taking the fifth will automatically result in a 0.0 score in both categories.

"We think using the difficulty and substance grades is important in assigning an overall score," continued Boehner. "After all, anybody should be able to get a 6.0 for substance on 1.0 difficulty questions like, 'State your name' or 'What state are you from?'. On the other hand, explaining a complex insurance exchange question is probably a 5.5 for difficulty so even a completely bullshit answer, if sincere, is probably worth two or three substance points. Of the major Obamacare testimony we've heard to date, based on scoring taped replays of the hearings, it's pretty clear that Health and Human Services Chief Technology Officer Todd Park has the lead with Health and Human Services Secretary Kathleen Sebelius a close second place."

Park, whose responses during his testimony were repeatedly interrupted by various Republican Representatives, commented, "Hey, anything that gets those Republicans to just shut up so that I can actually finish answering a question completely would be big improvement."

President Obama commented, "I'd really like to some comments because, as usual, I have a lot to say but since the testimony is under oath, on advice of counsel I regret to say that I have no comment."

Former President Bill Clinton commented, "I'm glad the House wasn't using this system back when I was testifying during my impeachment hearings. That French judge looks hot – uh – tough. Who knows how I would have scored with her?"

The House scoring rules will apply to testimony before all House committees. The U.S. Senate is expected to make a similar announcement regarding scoring rules for testimony before its committees later today.

◆ ◆ ◆

Hillary Clinton, Vladimir Putin and Hugo Chavez all die and find themselves in the anteroom of Hell awaiting their final sentence. While there, they notice an old style red dial telephone on the wall and they ask the Devil what the phone is for.

Says Satan, "The phone is for calling back to Earth but it is very expensive to use. Keep your calls short."

Putin asks to make one last call to Russia and talks for 5 minutes. When he is finished Satan informs him that the charges are 32 million rubles, so Putin writes him a check. Next, Chavez asks to make one last call to Venezuela and talks for 30 minutes. When he is finished Satan informs him that the cost is 37 million Venezuelan Bolívars, so Chavez writes him a check.

Finally, Hillary Clinton gets her turn, calls everybody on her phone list and talks for a total of over 6-1/2 hours. When she is finished, Satan informs her that the total cost for all the calls is $12.51.

When Putin and Chavez hear this they both go ballistic and demand that Satan explain why Clinton got to make multiple calls back to the U.S.A. for such low charges.

"Well," Satan replied with a broad smile, "Since Barack Obama took over as President the United States has gone to Hell, so instead of long distance now it's just a local call."

♦ ♦ ♦

At a medical conference four surgeons still managing to keep their medical practices running in spite of the arrival of Obamacare are discussing which patients are the easiest on which to perform surgery.

The first surgeon says, " I really think librarians are the easiest because everything inside them is in alphabetical order."

The second surgeon says, "I like operate on accountants because when you open them up, everything inside them is numbered."

The third surgeon says, "Nah, you ought to try operating on electricians. Everything inside them is color coded."

But the fourth surgeon disagreed, "You're all wrong. Politicians are by far the easiest to operate on. Thin skins, no hearts, no spines, no guts, no balls, big mouths and the heads and asses are interchangeable."

♦ ♦ ♦

Q.   What do politicians and baby diapers have in common?

A.   If you want to keep them clean, change them regularly.

♦ ♦ ♦

10 Things Obamacare Administrators Should Probably Not Say In Response To Senate Committee Questions:

10. "You call *THAT* a question? How the hell did *you* ever get elected?"

9. "I'm sorry but I can't answer that question because we're investigating ourselves."

8. "Please rephrase your question in the form of an answer..."

7. "I'm sorry Senator, I didn't say 'Simon says ask questions'. You're out."

6. "I'd love to answer that question but I've got a ferret in my shorts."

5. "You think that excuse was bad? Let me read this list of much worse excuses I *could* have used..."

4. "I'm taking the fifth...and while we're at it, could somebody please get me one?"

3. "Anybody here besides me think it's about time for a break?"

2. "I could answer that question, but then I'd have to kill you."

1. "You don't really think I'm going to answer that question honestly, do you?"

◆ ◆ ◆

Before the Obamacare rollout debacle, Senate Majority Leader Harry Reid (D-NV) was working in his office when his secretary informed him that he had two very important visitors waiting.

"Who are they?" asked Reid.

"Pope Francis and President Obama," replied his secretary.

"Send in the Pope first," sighed Reid, "I only have to kiss his ring."

◆ ◆ ◆

It was getting near closing time on Friday night at the Off The Record bar of elected officials, staffers and aides when an inebriated patron climbed up on a bar stool and shouted at the top of his lungs, "Politicians are just a bunch of dirty, low down, sneaky thieves."

There was an angry murmur from the collected politicians but it was Bernie Madoff who leapt to his feet and shouted back, "Hey, pal, I resent that remark."

Undeterred, the drunk shouted back "So, who are you, buddy, a politician??"

"No", said Madoff, "I'm a dirty, low down, sneaky thief."

◆ ◆ ◆

Obamacare has been tough on Democrat incumbents. On election night a member of the House of Representatives was sitting with his staff at his campaign headquarters awaiting the election returns when his iPhone rang. He answered and listened intently. After a brief moment, his face lit up with a smile.

"*Fox News* is projecting that we won!" he told his waiting staff. He immediately called his mother to pass along the good news.

"Mom, guess what? The election returns are in and despite my vote for Obamacare it looks like I won re-election!" he shouted joyously.

"Honestly?" replied his mother.

"Oh, Mom," he replied sheepishly, "Do you have to bring that up at a time like this?"

◆ ◆ ◆

10 Things Obama Administration Staffers Should Probably Not Do In Their Testimony Before Congressional Committees:

10. Present testimony using performance art.

9. Insist on right to trial by combat.

8. Begin any response with, "As a protest against the systematic and brutal oppression of women and minorities..."

7. Whine piteously, beg, cry, etc...

6. Espondray otay allway estionsquay inway Igpay Atinlay. ("Respond to all questions in Pig Latin.")

5. Leap up, slap committee chairman with a gauntlet and challenge him to a duel.

4. Threaten to toss anthrax filled envelope into an air conditioning vent.

3. Start talking in tongues.

2. Explode, implode or spontaneously combust.

1. Moon everyone in the room when finished.

◆ ◆ ◆

While driving home from the official White House ~~Christmas Holiday~~ Winter Festival party, a Senator and staunch Obamacare defender and his wife were pulled over by a Washington D.C. Metropolitan policeman. After examining the Senator's driver's license, proof of insurance and vehicle registration, the officer said, "Senator, do you realize that you were going over 70 mph in a 45 mph zone?"

"No way," replied the irritated Senator. "I don't think I was going over 50. Your radar must be out of calibration."

"Hah," said his wife, "My husband is a notorious speed demon. Everybody knows it. I thought we were going over 80!"

The Senator glares over at her but keeps his cool.

"Also, Senator," continued the officer, "I notice that you are not wearing your seat belt. That's an infraction here in Washington D.C. and I'm going to have to write you a ticket for that, too."

"Now wait a minute," said the Senator, becoming a bit more agitated. "I just unbuckled the seat belt when you pulled us over so I could get out my wallet to show you my driver's license."

"What a liar," said his wife. "He never wears his seat belt. I nag him about it all the time."

"DAMN IT, HONEY," yelled the upset Senator, losing his cool at last,. **"WILL YOU PLEASE JUST SHUT UP, SIT BACK AND LET ME HANDLE THIS!!!!"**

"Excuse me, Ma'am," interrupted the Metro policeman. "Is the Senator always this verbally abusive to you?"

"Why no, officer," replied his wife sweetly with a wicked smile, "Only when he's been drinking."

◆ ◆ ◆

How about that candidate running for the Senate who promised that if he was elected he'd introduce legislation that would guarantee that everybody would have an above average income?

◆ ◆ ◆

6.0   Media

During an appearance on ABC's *Good Morning America,* conservative pundit Charles Krauthammer was being interviewed by George Stephanopoulos. Stephanopoulos was being sharply critical of Republicans who criticize Obamacare without actually proposing a solution to replace it.

"C'mon Charles," said Stephanopoulos to Krauthammer, "While the Republicans have been very critical of Obamacare, they have yet to offer a comprehensive solution with which to replace it. Don't you think that before their criticisms and proposals to repeal or modify Obamacare are taken seriously that they should have to offer an alternative plan of their own?"

"Well, George," replied Krauthammer dryly after a few seconds of thought, "As I'm sure you know, it is recorded in Greek mythology that the fifth labor of Heracles was to clean from the stables of King Augeas the dung from his huge herd of over 1,000 cows. Nowhere is it recorded that he was required to refill the stables."

◆ ◆ ◆

Health and Human Services Secretary Kathleen Sebelius had just concluded a particularly intense session before the House Committee on Oversight and Government Reform investigating the Obamacare website development debacle. On the steps of the Senate she stopped to address a waiting gaggle of reporters, much to the horror of White House counsel Kathryn Ruemmler, who had just noticed that Representative Darrell Issa (R-CA), the powerful chairman of the committee, was standing nearby and listening intently to every word of Sebelius's diatribe.

"These redundant committees are just grandstanding for the press and being completely unfair," railed the irate Sebelius. "They are a bunch of headline seeking partisan hacks and computer software neophytes who have no idea what they're talking about. Most of them are lawyers for God's sake – talk about disconnected from reality!! This whole ridiculous witch hunt is nothing but a complete waste of time and money."

"You shouldn't take this too seriously," said Ruemmler, sidling up alongside Issa and trying valiantly to regain control of the situation, "When she gets worked up like this, Kathleen is sometimes really her own worst enemy."

"Not while I'm alive," replied Issa.

◆ ◆ ◆

A Soviet journalist stationed in Washington D.C. for *Pravda* walks into the emergency room at the Georgetown Medical Center and tells the admitting desk nurse, "I need to see an 'Eye-Ear' doctor."

"There is no such specialty," the nurse tells him. "Perhaps you would like to see another doctor?"

"No, I really need to see an 'Eye-Ear' doctor," the journalist says.

"But there are no such doctors," she replies, again. "Here, we have doctors for the eyes called 'ophthalmologists' and doctors who specialized in treating the ear, nose and throat, but there are no 'Eye-Ear' doctors."

Still no help. He repeats, "I need to see an 'Eye-Ear' doctor."

Finally the nurse gives up and calls the on-call attending physician who asks the Russian in Russian, "Comrade, we have no 'Eye-Ear' doctors, but if we did, why would you want to see one?"

"Because," the journalist replies, "I'm trying to cover Obamacare for my readers back home in Russia, but I keep hearing one thing with my ears and seeing something totally different with my eyes."

◆ ◆ ◆

Sean Hannity, Kirstin Powers and Rush Limbaugh were all on the same flight en route to New York when the airplane in which they were flying crashed. Hannity and Powers find themselves in the judgment hall of Purgatory, but Limbaugh is nowhere to be seen. After an interminable wait, each in turn approached the dais to hear their sentence.

"Sean Hannity," a basso profundo voice boomed, "In penance for your sins you are required to spend the next 10 years producing women's features for the *Lifetime* network; no political commentaries, no controversial stories, no hard news stories."

"Kirstin Powers," the voice continued, "In penance for your sins you are required to spend the next 20 years as a call screener for the Glenn Beck radio program; no political commentaries, no controversial stories, no hard news stories."

Leaving the judgment hall to begin their sentences, Hannity and Powers notice Rush Limbaugh in the adjoining hall handcuffed to MSNBC's Rachel Maddow. As they are about to ask the docent what's going on they hear the now familiar voice boom, "Rush Limbaugh, in penance for your sins...."

◆ ◆ ◆

We're not saying that the press is totally in the tank for President Obama but if Ben and Jerry's ever came up with a new flavor called "Obama's Butt" there are a large numbers of mainstream media reporters, columnists, pundits and bloggers who would never leave the ice cream parlor.

◆ ◆ ◆

President Barack Obama, Former President George W. Bush and New Jersey Governor Chris Christie are giving a joint news briefing when an asteroid strikes the podium and kills all three of them. Upon arriving in Heaven, the three of them are ushered in front of God's golden throne to justify their lives.

"Well," says God to Christie, "What have you done to justify entering Heaven?"

"I lived a good life, I was a good family man, I was a good Governor for my state of New Jersey and before that I fought political corruption as a federal prosecutor," replies Christie.

"Fine," replies God. "You may enter Heaven. You're next, Bush. What's your story?"

"Well," replies Bush, "I was President of the United States. I lowered taxes, improved education and fought international terrorism to make the world a safer place - and I did all this while the Democrats opposed my every move and the press made fun of my occasional errors in grammarification."

"Impressive," says God. "Come up here and sit beside me on my golden throne so that we can talk some more later. Now, what have you got to say for yourself, Obama?"

"I think....," replies President Obama, after thinking a minute, "That you're sitting in my seat."

♦ ♦ ♦

President Obama is seen walking across the waters of the Potomac River. Headlines the next day:

The New York Times:	"Divine Obama walks on water"
The Washington Post:	"President Obama confounds Republicans, walks across Potomac River"
The Wall Street Journal:	"President Obama finds rocky path across the Potomac River"

A week later former President George W. Bush is also seen walking across the waters of the Potomac River. Headlines the next day:

The Wall Street Journal:	"Former President Bush walks on water and saves taxpayers the cost of a boat"
The Washington Post:	"Former President Bush crosses the Potomac River on foot"
The New York Times:	"Former President Bush can't swim"

♦ ♦ ♦

News Headline: "Obamacare - 5 Important Things To Avoid!"

Hello! Do we really need four more?

♦ ♦ ♦

If Jay Carney breaks down and runs screaming from a White House Obamacare press briefing here are 10 possible replacement spokespeople*:

10. Frank Abagnale

9. Bozo the Clown

8. Cassandra

7. Harold Hill

6. Jack Kevorkian

5. Thomas Crown

4. Harcourt Fenton Mudd

3. Henry Gondorf

2. Bernie Madoff

1. Charles K. Ponzi

*See Chapter 9, "Who's Who," for the identities of these famous potential spokespeople.

◆ ◆ ◆

One afternoon, White House Press Secretary Jay Carney was taking a break to walk around the mall in Washington D.C. when he happened upon an old brass lamp. Tarnished and covered with weeds and Spanish moss, the lamp had clearly seen better days. As he sat down on a log and began polishing the lamp there was suddenly a bright blue flash and a small, rotund genie bearing an uncanny resemblance to Robert Reich popped into view amid a swirl of acrid smoke.

"I am the genie of the lamp," said the genie, "And as your reward for liberating me I will grant you three wishes. You must choose now. Know ye, however, that this lamp was once the property of Karl Rove. Whatsoever you ask of me I am obligated to grant to him two fold."

After thinking for a few minutes, Carney responded, "For my first wish I want one billion dollars deposited in my personal checking account."

"Your wish is my command. One billion dollars has been deposited in your personal checking account. Two billion dollars has also been deposited in Karl Rove's personal checking account."

"For my second wish," continued Carney, "When I arrive home I would like that red Ferrari 250 GTO that I have always wanted to be waiting for me in my driveway."

"Your wish is my command. The car you have wished for is now parked in the driveway at your home. Two red Ferraris are now parked in Karl Rove's driveway."

"This is my third and final wish," said Carney, "And I want you to listen <u>very</u> closely. I'm going to go walk from here to the Capital Hill Medical Center and check myself in. Once I'm safely there I want to have a heart attack that exactly half kills me."

"Your wish is my command," replied the genie.

◆ ◆ ◆

10 things you're not likely to hear President Obama say at a press conference about Obamacare:

10. "Wow, that was a really good question!"

9. "You're right. This may really be too expensive."

8. "I don't know enough to speak intelligently about that."

7. "Maybe I should have asked Kathleen Sebelius a few more questions about how the website development was progressing."

6. "I'll bet you I can get through this entire press conference without once saying, 'Let me be clear'."

5. "I'd like to stay and answer more questions but I've got a tee time at the Beverly Country Club - in Chicago."

4. "I'm going to have to check with Michelle and get back to you on that one."

3. "Boy, those guys at CGI Group sure knew their stuff. NOT!!"

2. "Oh, yeah, like I'm really going to admit that I screwed up! AS IF!!"

1. "Wow, this was the hard way to get you guys to quit asking questions about Benghazi."

♦ ♦ ♦

After spending a week in Washington D.C., Bill O'Reilly was preparing to board a plane back to New York when he heard that Pope Francis was on the same flight. "This is interesting," thought Bill, a devout Catholic. "I've always wanted to meet this new Pope. Very interesting fellow. Imagine, he flies commercial instead of taking a private plane. A true man of the people. Today I should be able to see him or maybe even talk to him in person about my newest book, *Killing Jesus*."

Imagine O'Reilly's surprise when the Holy Father sat down in the seat next to him for the flight. Shortly after takeoff, the Pope began a crossword puzzle. "This is fantastic," thought Bill. "I'm a whiz at crosswords. I do the *New York Times* crossword puzzle every Sunday. If he gets stuck, maybe he'll ask me to help."

Sure enough, almost immediately the Pope turned to O'Reilly and said, "Excuse me my son, but do you know a five letter word referring to a very unpleasant woman and that ends in the four letters 'i-t-c-h'?"

Only one word leapt to mind ... "Hmmm...," thought Bill, "I can't tell the Pope that. There must be another word." O'Reilly wracked his brain for a while then it hit him. Triumphant, he turned to the Pope and said, "Your Holiness, I think the word you're looking for is 'w-i-t-c-h'."

"Oooooh, of course!" replied the Pontiff. "Thank you my son. By the way, do you have an eraser?"

◆ ◆ ◆

After the disastrous rollout of the Obamacare website President Obama held a closed door briefing with top liberal reporters, pundits and bloggers to give out new talking points and encourage them to write more stories emphasizing the positive aspects of Obamacare. Later, Juan Williams was asked "Can you share with us how your meeting with the President went?" by Megyn Kelly of *Fox News*.

"Well," replied Williams, "The meeting was 'off the record' so I can't tell you exactly what was said. However, there was a very good discussion, lots of questions and a frank exchange of views. The bottom line is that we went into the meeting with our views and questions and we left with the Administration's views and the updated talking points we need to use now."

◆ ◆ ◆

A lonely congressional staffer new to Washington D.C. goes into the Eighteenth Street Lounge and sees a beautiful woman sitting alone on one of the couches. After an hour of gathering up his courage, he finally walks over to her and asks tentatively, "I'm new in town. Would you mind if I sat down and chatted with you for a while?"

To which she responds by jumping to her feet and yelling at the top of her lungs, "**NO, I WILL NOT SLEEP WITH YOU TONIGHT!**"

With everyone in the bar now staring at them, the staffer is embarrassed and humiliated so he quickly slinks back to his table. A few minutes later, the woman walks over to his table and apologizes. She smiles at him and says, "I'm really sorry if I embarrassed you. You see, I'm a writer for the Washington Post Lifestyles section and I've got an assignment to study how people in local bars respond to embarrassing situations."

To which he responds by jumping to his feet and yelling, at the top of his lungs, "**WHAT DO YOU MEAN, $200?**"

◆ ◆ ◆

Pundit George Will was on his way home from a meeting on Capitol Hill when he came to a dead halt in the traffic around Dupont Circle. He noticed a Metro police officer walking between the lines of stopped cars, so he rolled down his window and asked, "Officer, what's the hold-up?"

The officer replied, "President Obama is so depressed that he stopped his motorcade up ahead and is threatening to douse himself with gasoline and set himself on fire. He says no one believes his administration's explanations about Obamacare, the Iranian nuke deal, Benghazi, Syria, the IRS, the NSA, Fast and Furious, etc. He also thinks that the Republicans are always grossly distorting his entire record while obstructing his every move for political gain. And now his fellow Democrats are panicking before the mid-term elections and even the press corps is starting to turn on him. He's afraid nobody cares and he is just not sure he can carry on. We're taking up a collection for him to show him that people really do care."

Will asks, "How much have you collected so far?"

The officer replies, "Right around 12 gallons but a lot of folks are still siphoning."

♦ ♦ ♦

It has been reported that on his nationally syndicated radio show famous talk show host Rush Limbaugh called Obamacare, "...Essentially a computer virus". However, with all due respect to Rush, Obamacare really does not meet the definition of a virus. There are fundamental differences: Viruses are fast, compact, efficient, machine independent, robust and stable. Since this is clearly not true of Obamacare, it really cannot be a virus. It is more accurately a *plague*.

♦ ♦ ♦

Q.	How many journalists does it take to change a light bulb?

A.	Four. One to change the bulb, one liberal reporter to report changing the bulb as a continuation of a progressive program bringing the poor the light denied them by the heartless Republicans, one conservative reporter to report changing the bulb as a Democrat plot to deprive people of their Constitutional right to live in the dark and one blogger to report a secret conspiracy by light bulb manufacturers to break old style filament light bulbs so people will have no choice but to buy the newer, more expensive compact fluorescent bulbs.

♦ ♦ ♦

7.0   Obamapourri

If Barack Obama had been the Captain of the Titanic he would have told the passengers, "Don't worry, folks - we're just stopping to take on ice!"

♦ ♦ ♦

In spite of all the difficulties in his second term, President Obama decides to throw a grand New Year's Eve party at the White House. During the party he grabs the microphone and announces to his guests that he has had the White House swimming pool stocked with two great white sharks and a couple hundred piranhas. "I will award the Presidential Medal of Freedom, the highest civilian award in the land, to any person who has the courage to swim across that pool."

There are no takers so the party continues until suddenly there is a great splash down by the pool. When all the guests run to poolside to find out what has happened they see Kathleen Sebelius swimming as hard as she can for the far side of the pool. Fins are flashing, jaws are snapping and the water is frothing but Sebelius just keeps on paddling. Just as the sharks are about to overtake her she reaches the far side of the pool and clambers out; tired and wet, with a few piranhas hanging off her, she is otherwise unharmed.

Overwhelmed by this demonstration of courage, the President again grabs the microphone and says, "I am a man of my word. Kathleen, even though the launch of Obamacare was less than stellar I am ready to award you the Presidential Medal of Freedom for that was undoubtedly the bravest act I have ever seen."

Obama is still talking when the still dripping wet Sebelius grabs the microphone out of his hand and yells, "First, let's find Joe Biden. HE'S THE ONE WHO SHOVED ME IN!"

♦ ♦ ♦

There is no truth to the rumor that President Obama was overheard saying, "I'd kill for a Nobel Peace prize".

♦ ♦ ♦

On a foggy evening President Obama was on the bridge of the Arleigh Burke-class guided missile destroyer USS Barry (DDG-52) sailing off the coast of Virginia when he noticed the light of another ship directly ahead. At Obama's order, the Captain had the Barry's communications officer warn off the other ship, "Oncoming ship, this is the USS Barry. Please divert your course 10 degrees south to avoid a possible collision."

The polite response was immediate: "Acknowledged, Barry. We recommend you divert YOUR course 10 degrees north to avoid a possible collision."

Irritated, the President ordered the Captain to have a sterner warning issued: "This is the USS Barry. We have the right of way. I say again, divert **YOUR** course 10 degrees south to avoid a possible collision."

Again, the polite response was immediate: "Acknowledged, Barry. We say again, we recommend you divert **YOUR** course 10 degrees north to avoid a possible collision."

Obama was outraged. Snatching the microphone from the surprised communications officer's hand he shouted: **"This Is President Barack Obama Aboard The Destroyer USS Barry. I'm President Of The United States and The Commander In Chief. I <u>Always</u> Have The Right Of Way. I Never Change Course and I Brake For Nobody. I Order You To Divert Your Course South <u>Immediately</u> To Avoid A Collision!"**

The polite response remained unruffled: "Acknowledged, Mr. President. This is the Cape Henry lighthouse. Your call."

♦ ♦ ♦

Q.   Why is President Obama's Air Force One an aerodynamic miracle?

A.   The aircraft only has a left wing.

♦ ♦ ♦

10 Things about himself Barack Obama would rather you did NOT know about him:

10. Secretly watches all episodes of *Duck Dynasty*.

9. Has a complete collection of *Spiderman* comic books.

8. Actually can't lift the printed full text of the Obamacare law and regulations.

7. Major case of athletes foot.

6. After the 2012 election tweeted a selfie of himself in the oval office to Mitt Romney.

5. Has the words "Mt. Rushmore" on his bucket list. And he doesn't mean just a visit.

4. Secretly twerks in front of full length mirror in the White House master bedroom.

3. Has casually encouraged his supporters to investigate repealing the 22nd Amendment, "Just in case."

2. Actually never read the Affordable Care Act before or after signing it.

1. Sneaks over to the Pentagon at night dressed up like Darth Vader so he can fly live Predator drone missions over Afghanistan.

◆ ◆ ◆

While sailing the Presidential yacht in Chesapeake Bay, President Obama fell overboard. After paddling around for a while, he was picked up by a young man in a small sailboat.

Safely on board, Obama expressed his gratitude, "Thanks for saving me. I'm Barack Obama, President of the United States, the world's most powerful man. Name a reward and it's yours."

Thinking for a minute, the young man replied, "I'd like to have a really cool funeral and afterwards a major party for all my friends."

Pondering the odd request, Obama asked for clarification, "A fancy funeral seems like a pretty odd request for someone your age. Isn't there something else more appropriate that you want?"

"Well," replied the young man, "It's just that my father is self-employed and he and all his employees lost their health insurance when Obamacare went into effect. When they find out that I saved you from drowning, they're going to kill me!!"

◆ ◆ ◆

Sometime after the end of his term as President, Barack Obama dies and finds himself outside the Pearly Gates. Saint Peter then informs him that he is just on the edge of good enough for Heaven or bad enough for Hell so he will be allowed to choose between spending an eternity in Heaven or in Hell. Obama, dead but no fool, asks if he can look around both places before making a final decision.

"Very well," says Saint Peter. " Let's start with Hell."

There is immediately a bright flash of light and they are transported to the nether regions. When the smoke clears, Obama is surprised to see blue sky and beautiful beaches. A marimba band is playing in the background. There are gorgeous women in revealing swimsuits. A great buffet is laid out. He sees lots of his former friends from the DNC chatting down by the pool. There's a 36 hole golf course. The place has all the trappings of a world class resort.

"Very impressive," enthuses Obama, thinking to himself that if this is Hell, the downside of being dead must be pretty limited.

"Now, let's check out Heaven," said Saint Peter.

Another bright flash of light and they are transported back to the ethereal plane. A soft white light glows everywhere. There are discussion groups debating various aspects of political theory. A heavenly choir is singing joyous praises to God. Everyone is wearing comfortable unisex leisure suits. It looks and sounds like Oral Roberts University.

"Well," says Saint Peter, "It's time for you to choose."

"No offense," says Obama after a moment of thought, "But based upon what I've seen, I think I'll take Hell."

There is a final flash of light and Obama is stunned to find himself chained hip deep in a pool of molten lava while a line of Republicans stretching off into the distance wait to use a variety of nasty sharp edged and pointed implements to cut, poke and prod him in a variety of very tender places.

When Obama screams in pain for help, Saint Peter re-appears.

"What's the problem?" asks Saint Peter.

"What's the problem???" Shrieks Obama. **"This isn't what you showed me. Where is the pool, the beach, the golf course, the buffet, the babes????"**

"Ah," smiled Saint Peter, "Before, we were campaigning. Now, you've voted."

◆ ◆ ◆

President Obama, Vice President Joe Biden and Attorney General Eric Holder go out to lunch. While walking by a construction site in downtown Washington D.C. they saw a dirty, dented brass lamp lying next to a trench. Curious, Holder picked it up and gave it a rub. Instantly, there was a bright flash and a genie appeared. At first glance Holder thought that the genie looked decidedly like a blue tinted version of *The Five's* Greg Gutfeld but he was not really sure.

"OK, you all know the drill," said the genie, "Three wishes. But since there are three of you, you only get one wish each."

"Great!!" said Holder. "Send me to Hawaii forever with a beautiful woman."

POOF!! There was a bright flash of light, a puff of blue smoke and he was gone.

"Now me, Now me!!" said Biden. "Send me to Tahiti forever with two beautiful women."

POOF!! As before, there was a bright flash of light, a puff of blue smoke and he was gone.

The genie then turned to President Obama. "OK, it's your turn now. What do you want?"

Thinking a minute, the President smiled, "I want those two back in their offices and working at their desks right now."

♦ ♦ ♦

We'd never say that President Obama lied about the Affordable Care Act aka "Obamacare" when he said, "If you like your healthcare plan, you can keep it. Period." and other similar quotes but when IBM fed his collected quotes into the Pinocchio simulation running on their newest BS9000 neural net supercomputer the result was a wooden nose long enough to compete in the pole vault!

♦ ♦ ♦

A President name of Obama
Tried to govern with minimum drama.
With healthcare alas,
He fell on his ass
Causing Democrats everywhere trauma.

♦ ♦ ♦

We've heard that President Obama has amazing will power and is actually very spiritual. He recently skipped the Novocain during a root canal because he wanted to transcend dental medication.

♦ ♦ ♦

It's been a rough year for President Obama. One evening after a particularly difficult round of press conferences followed by a long evening of fund raisers he asked his wife, "Michelle, this is really wearing me down. If I just chucked it all, retired and gave up all of my political power would you still love me?"

"Of course I would," replied Michelle sweetly, "and I'd *miss* you, too."

◆ ◆ ◆

President Obama was out jogging with his Secret Service detail one morning when he noticed a little boy on a street corner with a box. Curious, the President jogged over to the child and said, "What do you have in that box, kid?"

The little boy replied, "Kittens, sir. It's a litter of newborn baby kittens."

Obama laughs and said, "What kind of kittens are they?"

"They're all Democrats, sir." the little boy replied.

"Oh, that's cute," said the President as he jogged on his way.

A couple days later Obama was jogging the same route, this time with his buddy Eric Holder. There, on the same corner, he spotted the same boy with his box of kittens. Thinking that maybe this time he'd take a kitten home for his daughters, he headed over to the corner again.

"You need to check out these cute kittens," said the President as he and Holder jogged over to the little boy with his box. "Hey, kid, tell my friend Eric what kind of kittens they are."

But this time the boy replied, "They're all Republicans."

"Now wait a minute!", said the surprised President. "When I came by here just a couple days ago you said that the kittens were all Democrats. What's going on?"

"Well, Mr. President," the boy nervously replied after some hesitation, "Their eyes are open now."

◆ ◆ ◆

Back before it became clear that there were going to be major problems with Obamacare, President Obama and former Chief of Staff Rahm Emanuel were at a planning session at Camp David. During a break one afternoon they were out hiking in the woods when they found their path blocked by a huge grizzly bear. They reversed course immediately but were dismayed to find that the bear was following them and looking most unfriendly. The President quickly stopped, took off his daypack, removed his mountain hiking boots and started to put on his running shoes.

"Mr. President," said Emanuel, "This is stupid. Forget it. I know you're in great shape but we can't possibly outrun a grizzly bear. Let's just call the Secret Service and have them shoot it."

"Rahm," said the Obama, "The Secret Service may not get here in time. Anyway, I don't have to outrun the bear. I just have to outrun you."

◆ ◆ ◆

President Obama, feeling a bit overwhelmed by the stresses of the job, decided to see the White House psychiatrist. The psychiatrist had him get comfortable on the couch then began the session.

"Since we've never met before," said the doctor, "I'm not sure what is bothering you. Perhaps you should tell me about your problem starting at the very beginning."

"Of course," replied the President. "In the beginning, I created the Heavens and the Earth..."

◆ ◆ ◆

Q.   How many members of the Obama administration does it take to change a light bulb?

A.   None. "Hope and Change" was supposed to take care of it.

◆ ◆ ◆

We heard that President Obama pardoned a turkey for Thanksgiving. We've been unable to confirm whether this was a bird or the chief architect of the Healthcare.gov website.

◆ ◆ ◆

10 Things NOT to tell President Obama at the Obamacare review meeting:

10. "Blue Cross / Blue Shield just cancelled another 15 million insurance policies."

9. "The healthcare.gov database has been hacked and all insurance enrollment data to date uploaded to wikileaks."

8. "We need to call the teleprompter repair guy again."

7. "Hackers just redirected the heathcare.gov home page to www.houseofpain.com."

6. "Uh, we've got the latest poll numbers from Gallup....."

5. "Bo the dog just had a little accident under the Resolute desk."

4. "The White House healthcare plan was just cancelled for not complying with the new Obamacare regulations."

3. "Harry Reid called to tell you that the Senate just voted to exempt itself and all of its staff members from enrolling in Obamacare."

2. "Politifact is calling on line 1 about giving you another award."

1. "Have you heard that great new joke about Obamacare?"

◆ ◆ ◆

President Obama was invited to throw out the first pitch at the Washington National's first baseball game of the new season. Since First Lady Michelle Obama is not really a baseball fan, the President attended with former Speaker of the House Nancy Pelosi.

As the crowd roared, the umpire walked to the Presidential box and yelled something up to the President. Suddenly, President Obama leaped to his feet, grabbed a startled Pelosi by the collar and, summoning up all of his strength, heaved her up and over the railing onto the field below.

"No, NO, Mr. President!" shouted the stunned umpire. "I said, 'It's time for you to throw out the first PITCH!'"

◆ ◆ ◆

Stepping out of the shower in the White House master bathroom one morning, President Obama slipped on the wet tile and fell to the floor with a loud 'thud'.

"OH MY GOD, are you all right," screamed his wife.

"Michelle, dear," said the President as he staggered to his feet rubbing his head, "When we're alone you know you can just call me 'Barack'."

◆ ◆ ◆

Valerie Jarrett rushed into the Oval Office. "Mr. President, I've got good news and I've got bad news."

"What's the good news?" asked the President.

"A new Gallup poll found that almost 41 percent of Americans think Obamacare might really be a good thing for them after all!" replied Jarrett

"And the bad news?" asked the President.

"Unfortunately," said Jarrett after a pause, "That same poll found that more than 55 percent can't afford to pay for the coverage."

◆ ◆ ◆

10 recent Barack Obama impulse purchases:

10. "Thinking of You" card for George W. Bush

9. iPhone lessons

8. Kevlar basketball shorts

7. Copy of *Website Development for Dummies*

6. "Better Luck Next Time" card for Mitt Romney

5. Obedience school lessons for Bo the dog.

4. GPS trackers for both daughters

3. Teleprompter cozy

2. Rush Limbaugh voodoo doll

1. Cliff Notes® version of The Affordable Care and Patient Protection Act

♦ ♦ ♦

A clockmaker died and went to heaven. As he stood in front of the Pearly Gates waiting for Saint Peter he was surprised to see a wall of odd looking clocks stretching off into the distance.

When Saint Peter arrived the clockmaker asked, "What are all those odd looking clocks?"

Saint Peter answered, "Those are 'lie clocks'. Every person on Earth has a lie clock that starts running when they are born. Throughout their lives every time they tell a lie, the hands on their lie clock moves."

"Oh," said the clockmaker, noticing that one of the clocks appears to be stopped. "Whose clock is that? It looks broken."

"That's Mother Teresa's. The hands never moved, indicating that she never told a lie in her entire life."

"That's incredible," said the clockmaker. He pointed to another clock.

"That's Abraham Lincoln's clock. The hands were moved twice, telling us that Honest Abe told only two lies in his entire life," Saint Peter informed him.

More curious than ever, the clockmaker asked, "Where's President Obama's lie clock?"

Saint Peter looked around furtively and whispered, "You know, I'm really not supposed to say anything, but President Obama's clock isn't up here any more. After that whole, 'If you like your insurance you can keep your insurance' thing, his lie clock was moved, uh, 'down below', if you know what I mean and You-Know-Who has been using it as a ceiling fan ever since."

♦ ♦ ♦

One night, President Obama was having a tough time getting to sleep. After tossing and turning he got out of bed and took a walk around the White House. As he passed by the portrait of George

Washington he muttered, "What is the best thing I could do to help the country?" and he was surprised to hear a faint but clear voice whispering from the portrait, "Set an honest and honorable example, just as I did," Washington advised.

As he continued on he came to the portrait of Thomas Jefferson and asked the same question, "What is the best thing I could do to help the country?" and he heard another faint response from the portrait, "Go to the people, just as I did," Jefferson advised.

Finally, Obama arrived at the portrait of Lincoln and again asked his question, "What is the best thing I could do to help the country?" and he heard another whispered response from the portrait, "Go to the theater, just as I did," Lincoln advised.

◆ ◆ ◆

Q. How do you get to Obamaville?

A. Take a sharp left turn and it's all downhill from there.

◆ ◆ ◆

Obama is our shepherd, We shall all want.

2: He maketh us to use only green products. He leadeth us beside the dead businesses.

3: He destroyeth our jobs. He stalleth the Keystone pipeline for environmental extremist's sake.

4: Yea, though we crawl through this recession unending we shall fear no evil. For thou art with us; My Obamaphone and my EBT card they comfort me.

5: Thou expandeth food stamps and EPA regulations to levels never seen. Thou burdeneth us with Obamacare. Our taxes runneth over.

6: Surely a lower standard of living shall be ours all the rest of our lives and our unemployed children shall dwell in our house forever.

Amen

◆ ◆ ◆

And finally....

President Obama, tiring of Obamacare being the butt of so many jokes, unleashes the FBI, NSA and IRS to locate the source. After an exhaustive search, they locate the author of the jokes and the President decides to confront him in person.

"Are you responsible for that stupid joke about me ending up in Hell after selecting it during a political campaign?" Obama demanded.

"Yes, sir, Mr. President."

"How about the ridiculous one where the boy saves me from drowning and is afraid his father will kill him for saving me??"

"Mine, too."

"What about that really lame one about my wanting to take God's golden throne???"

"Mine, again."

"HOW DARE YOU WRITE ALL THIS CRAP YOU PRESUMPTUOUS NOBODY??" yells the President, going ballistic. **"I'm Barack Obama, the President of the United States. I'm the most powerful man in the world. Before I'm through, Obamacare will be providing great health insurance coverage to millions of Americans who were without health insurance, improving the health insurance coverage for millions more Americans who already had health insurance coverage and all the while bending the cost curve for the nation's healthcare spending lower and. . ."**

"Now wait a minute, Mr. President," said the joker, interrupting the President's tirade. "That last one isn't mine...."

◆ ◆ ◆

8.   BONUS CHAPTER – OBAMACARE Late Night

Any President knows he's on thin ice when his signature piece of legislation becomes a regular target for late night comedians. Well, Obamacare made it, big time! Here are some of the best:

"According to CBS News, only six people enrolled in Obamacare on the first day of the rollout. Six! That means more people have walked on the moon than have signed up for Obamacare." - Jay Leno on *The Tonight Show*

"Anybody try to sign up for the Obamacare? It's impossible, and everybody's furious. The Republicans are upset about Obamacare because something they tried to stop now won't get started." - David Letterman on *The Late Show with David Letterman*

"The Obama administration asks Hollywood to work positive mentions of Obamacare into its TV shows and movies. So AMCs new zombie drama is titled: "The Walking Dead but Not Due to Preexisting Conditions." - Conan O'Brien on *Conan*

"The White House now says the Obamacare website will be fixed by the end of November. So if your doctor has only given you three weeks to live, sorry pal." - Jay Leno on *The Tonight Show*

"So, yes, the President was somewhat dishonest about the promise of his healthcare program, but here's the weird part, his opponents have been lying like motherfuckers about its effects" - Jon Stewart on the *The Daily Show*

"There was some good news today for embattled Health and Human Services Secretary Kathleen Sebelius. Obamacare will cover all her injuries after the White House throws her under the bus. She is totally covered." - Jay Leno on *The Tonight Show*

"In Nevada, where prostitution is legal - true story - prostitutes are signing up for Obamacare. Which explains why the most popular pick-up line in Nevada is, 'Let me help you with your co-pay.'" - Conan O'Brien on *Conan*

"The Republicans in Congress voted to repeal Obamacare for a fortieth time today. It's really now less a governing philosophy; it's more like Charlie Manson applying for parole." - Bill Maher on *Real Time with Bill Maher*

"According to a new report, more than 700 fake Obamacare websites have been created. Security experts say it's simple to identify the phony sites because they are easy to log on to." - Jay Leno on *The Tonight Show*

"Obama is wrestling with the healthcare rollout debacle. He urged Americans not to be put off by the Obamacare website and offered alternative ways to enroll, such as using the mail. Then the president got on his horse and rode off to spread the news to the next town." - Conan O'Brien on *Conan*

"When Bill Clinton is lecturing you on your commitments, that's when it gets a little testy" - Jay Leno on *The Tonight Show*

"Your chances of winning the big lottery are 250 million to 1. It's the same as your chance of getting on the Obamacare website. It's virtually impossible." - David Letterman on *The Late Show with David Letterman*

"A friend of mine was given six months by his doctor. Not to live - to sign up for Obamacare." - Jay Leno on *The Tonight Show*

"Obama said they've had some glitches with the Affordable Care website. I'll tell you something. If you order a pair of pants online and they send you the wrong color, that's a glitch. This is like a Carnival cruise, for God's sake!" - David Letterman on *The Late Show with David Letterman*

"President Obama said he is sorry that some Americans have lost their existing health coverage due to Obamacare. I think he's getting a little desperate. Today he said if you like your complete lack of coverage, you can keep your complete lack of coverage." - Jay Leno on *The Tonight Show*

"Many scam artists are trying to take advantage of the problems with the Obamacare website. Experts say you can tell it's a scam site if you enter your information and it quickly and efficiently signs you up for healthcare." - Conan O'Brien on *Conan*

"The CEO of The Cheesecake Factory is now warning that Obamacare will be very costly. Hey, The Cheesecake Factory is one of the reasons we need Obamacare in the first place." - Jay Leno on *The Tonight Show*

"Today the White House confirmed that Obama will be signing up for Obamacare. Yeah, which is good because his current health plan doesn't cover headaches and depression caused by Obamacare." - Conan O'Brien on *Conan*

"This things gotten so crazy, the Rev. Wright lost his health care and blamed the Jews." - Dennis Miller on *The O'Reilly Factor*

"The Obama White House website still says if you like your health plan, you can keep it. That's false, of course. The President says they're trying to correct it, but his website people can't seem to log on." - Jay Leno on *The Tonight Show*

"President Obama's approval rating is down to 39 percent. And Toronto Mayor Rob Ford, who admitted to smoking crack cocaine, went up to 49 percent. How does this make Obama feel? He'd be better off smoking crack than passing Obamacare." - Jay Leno on *The Tonight Show*

"The CEO of the Olive Garden blames his company's low profits on Obamacare – which is odd because most people won't eat at the Olive Garden until they have health insurance." - Conan O'Brien on *Conan*

"It [Obamacare] is a dysfunctional mess, no one is denying that. But don't worry, Congress is on the case. The Republicans held hearings yesterday. They are outraged that the thing they did not want to work is not working." - Bill Maher on *Real Time with Bill Maher*

"Obama and other Democrats have even stopped using the term 'Obamacare,' when referring to the new healthcare law. Yeah, now they're calling it 'the Affordable Care Act.' Americans were like, 'Just let us know when you can call it 'fixed.''" - Jimmy Fallon on *Late Night with Jimmy Fallon*

"According to insiders, the White House hired a consulting firm that told them the Obamacare website wasn't ready. But the White House went ahead. The White House made this mistake because they don't know how to open their email." - David Letterman on *The Late Show with David Letterman*

"Did you know the speeches he's [President Obama's] made about affordable health care is greater than the number of people who have signed up for it?"- Jimmy Kimmel on *Jimmy Kimmel Live!*

"According to a report out today, over one million Californians are losing their health insurance due to Obamacare. In fact, some of them are so angry they've already gone back to Mexico." - Jay Leno on *The Tonight Show*

"President Obama is urging Americans who are having trouble with the Obamacare website to sign up by calling an 800 number. The number is 1-800-'We Didn't Think This Through'." - Conan O'Brien on *Conan*

"You can also enroll over the phone. The call goes like this: 'Hello and welcome to Healthcare.gov, the place where you can learn about signing up for affordable healthcare. Right now there are eight million people ahead of you in line. Your estimated wait time is forever.' It would be ironic to die while waiting on hold for health insurance, right?."- Jimmy Kimmel on *Jimmy Kimmel Live!*

"How many of you are only here because you had some trouble signing up for Obamacare and instead you got tickets for this show?" - David Letterman on *The Late Show with David Letterman*

"Americans have waited seventy years for affordable healthcare, but if the website takes more than an hour, fuck it, I'm watching a cat video. Some people said they had to sit at their computers for up to nine straight hours, beating the old record set by Anthony Weiner." - Bill Maher on *Real Time with Bill Maher*

"This techno-turd taco will be Barack Obama's true legacy. It's his Gettysburg address if Lincoln had said, 'Four score and . . . Error 404 . . . emancipation not found'..." - Stephen Colbert on *The Colbert Report*

"Despite all of the website problems, the approval rating for Obamacare has gone up. Unfortunately, I can't give you the exact number because it's listed on the Obamacare website." - Conan O'Brien on *Conan*

"Mr. President, if you liked your apology, YOU CAN KEEP IT!" - Dennis Miller on *The O'Reilly Factor*

"President [Obama] is like a man who burns your house down and then shows up with an empty water bucket and then delivers a lecture on how bad your house was before he burned it down." - Representative Steve Scalise (R-LA)

"If you are in need of healthcare, you have two choices. You can wait for them to get the website fixed or you can enroll in medical school, graduate and take care of yourself - which is probably faster."- Jimmy Kimmel on *Jimmy Kimmel Live!*

"So far, only 106,000 people have signed up for Obamacare. Even more disappointing is that it turned out to be one man who accidentally signed up 106,000 times" - David Letterman on *The Late Show with David Letterman*

"For years President Obama has been saying that no one would lose their healthcare plan. Now the White House has admitted that in fact many people will lose their plans. But there is a way to keep the great coverage you have. Just become a member of

Congress. Then the taxpayers pay for the whole thing." - Jay Leno on *The Tonight Show*

"The Obamacare website won't be accessible at night due to maintenance. And it won't be accessible during the day due to it sucking." - Conan O'Brien on *Conan*

"Obamacare needs the premiums of healthier people to cover the costs of sicker people. It's a devious con that can only be described as 'insurance'..." - Stephen Colbert on *The Colbert Report*

"The White House just announced that it is bringing in the best and brightest tech experts to fix the glitches on the Obamacare website, which is a great plan. You know what would have been a better plan? Hiring the best and brightest tech experts to make the Obamacare website in the first place." - Jimmy Fallon on *Late Night with Jimmy Fallon*

"President Obama and his top aides met with insurance company CEOs at the White House on Friday. So we've got politicians meeting with insurance salesmen. You know, if you throw in a couple of used car dealers, you have the trifecta of professional lying right there." - Jay Leno on *The Tonight Show*

"President Obama is being criticized for not attending today's ceremony commemorating the Gettysburg Address. In fairness, though, Lincoln did not attend Obama's 'Sorry about this crappy website' speech." - Conan O'Brien on *Conan*

"The president said despite the initial problems, it's [Obamacare website's] working better now and going do continue to improve. A million people visited on Monday, mostly to see if they were covered from injuries suffered at Wal-Mart on Black Friday."- Jimmy Kimmel on *Jimmy Kimmel Live!*

◆ ◆ ◆

9. Who's Who

Names, titles and starting page numbers of items featuring these famous characters:

◆ ◆ ◆

About the Author/Editor

Tim Barry has been in and around the personal computer industry since 1974. Starting out as a semiconductor engineer at legendary semiconductor pioneer Fairchild Semiconductor, his career in Silicon Valley spanned the start up of the personal computer and Internet eras and included a variety of positions in hardware/software product development, consulting and senior management.

The holder of eight patents; the author of five books plus numerous articles on the personal computer industry, the editor of over 50 computer books and a former *Infoworld* columnist, Mr. Barry is currently the President and CEO of Intelligent Technologies, Inc., an Internet consulting firm he founded in 1998 that also operates a number of niche market ecommerce stores under it's ITI Web Stores brand (www.itiwebstores.com). In his spare time he plays the piano, consults, writes, serves on boards of directors and bores his friends with tales of the halcyon years of the personal computer industry.

A long time collector of jokes and other humorous material, Mr. Barry is also an amateur stand up comedian. *The Totally Unauthorized Obamacare Joke Book* ™, is the fourth in his series of *Totally Unauthorized Joke Books* ™. The first three members of the series were *The Totally Unauthorized Microsoft Joke Book* ™, *The Totally Unauthorized Microsoft Joke Book* ™, *2nd Edition* and *The Totally Unauthorized Enron Joke Book* ™. All are collections of topical jokes, top 10 lists, original poems and other humorous material.

◆ ◆ ◆

www.ingramcontent.com/pod-product-compliance
Lightning Source LLC
Chambersburg PA
CBHW071640050426
42443CB00026B/794

9780966741735